THREE
PLAYS

WAYNE STATE UNIVERSITY PRESS DETROIT in association

with HEINEMAN EDUCATIONAL BOOKS NIGERIA PLC

TESS AKAEKE ONWUEME

THREE
PLAYS

The Broken Calabash

Parables for a Season

The Reign of Wazobia

AFRICAN AMERICAN LIFE SERIES

A complete listing of the books in this series can be found at the back of this volume.

General Editors

TONI CADE BAMBARA *Author and Filmmaker*

GENEVA SMITHERMAN *Michigan State University*

WILBUR C. RICH *Wellesley College*

RONALD W. WALTERS *Howard University*

The introduction originally appeared in Drumvoices Revue: A Confluence of Literary, Cultural & Vision Arts, vol. 1, nos. 1 and 2 (Fall-Winter 1991/92). Reprinted by permission.
Correspondence by Kendall used by permission.
The Broken Calabash copyright © 1984, 1988 by Tess Akaeke Onwueme.
The Reign of Wazobia copyright © 1988 by Tess Akaeke Onwueme.
Published under license in North America by Wayne State University Press.

LIBRARY OF CONGRESS CATALOGING-IN-PUBLICATION DATA
Onwueme, Tess Akaeke.
  (Selections. 1993)
  Three plays / by Tess Akaeke Onwueme.
      p.   cm.—(African American life series)
  Contents: The broken calabash—Parables for a season—The reign of Wazobia.
  ISBN 0-8143-2444-4 (alk. paper)—ISBN 0-8143-2445-2 (pbk. : alk. paper)
  1. Nigeria—Drama. I. Title. II. Series.
PR9387.9.O537A6   1993
822—dc20
                                                                92-47582

DESIGNER | COVER ART: S.R. TENENBAUM

FOR THEM WHO WHET MY TONGUE ON THE SHARP EDGE OF TRUTH—my father, Chief Jụlụga Adaka-Akaeke, Ine-o! The beauty of Ọgwashi-uku! Édé-O! Awali-ego! Ine, nnam! Ugbana-nwa ézé ọcha! Édé! Ine! Awaili! Édé! Okọcha ugbana! Édé-o! Affàà-a! Ọnụ-ekwulu ọha! Édé!–and my husband, Innocent Chukwuma Onwueme, Oje-ọba! Oje-ọba! Oje-ọba sugé! Nwata-dike! Nwa-Onwueme ogbu asụkwụ! Nwa-onye ukala enwe! Ndiji azụ ụkwụ adàà ọfia! Oje-ọba! Utọmi na awele!

Contents

Foreword

Tess Akaeke Onwueme writes to purge herself of oppressive feelings, and her plays serve that important function for all of us. They not only bring us the range and beauty of Nigerian culture, but speak to the heart of people everywhere. Her works examine the intersection of tradition and ritual, as well as the construction of gender, and though her framework is particular to Nigeria, her dramas are pertinent to oppressed peoples of all countries as well as the United States—particularly women. Indeed, her dramatic works create an artistic bridge crucial to international understanding of human rights for all, everywhere. It is fortunate that North American readers can now have the benefit of finding, under one cover, three of those anthologized for the first time.

The Broken Calabash had its U.S. premiere at the Bonstelle Theatre, Wayne State University in Detroit, where the playwright spent a year in residency as guest writer. The drama attracted a large crowd because of its relevance to the theme of black identity. It is a significant tragedy which was originally produced by the Federal University of Technology, Owerri Theatre Troupe at the National Theatre, Iganmu Lagos, in October, 1984. This led to the National Television Authority production of a film version in December 1985.

The play constitutes an intellectual revolt against the decadent traditional values of a caste system. It portrays the triumph of love over the inhumanity of discrimination and raises the important question of modern Nigerian women's subjugation to outmoded traditions. It shows the tragic consequences of denying any human being, female or male, the right to an individual life of self-fulfillment.

"We live in a society where women have it very hard," says the playwright. "Their lives are manipulated by others." The protagonists of Dr. Tess Onwueme's plays tend to be women who revolt against their misuse by an outdated and inhumane system.

These are themes which can be understood from the United States to Eastern Europe, today, from China or India, to Latin America or Africa. According to the widely-heralded report, *The World's Women*, from the United Nations (1990), the plight of women is universally similar. To one degree or another it involves levels of oppression not experienced by males. We North American women can remind ourselves of the fact that our mothers and grandmothers only achieved the right to vote in their lifetime. The women of that generation still alive today are a living representation of suffragette history. Also, more than 90 percent of U.S. women are in the work force, not out of feminist choice, but the need to put bread on the tables of their families. They must nurture their children and survive in the work force, often without a decent childcare system or adequate health care, let alone equal pay for equal work or a work place free of sexual harassment. These sociological reasons allow us North Americans to identify strongly with the women in Tess Onwueme's plays. Their themes are far more universal than they might appear at first glance. Her dramas are very much universal plays for an international audience as they speak to us of basic human rights regardless of nationality, age, sex, or race.

The mother of five children, Onwueme says that "writing is like giving birth." But, she adds, "If love drove me to childbirth, alienation drove me to writing, and love for portraying truth drove me to continue writing. . . . I happen to come from the Igbo ethnic group in my country, and the social and political conditions in the country have created my ideological perspective. I feel that the role of any writer is to develop consciousness in the audience. We are not just writing for entertainment alone. There's enough entertainment going on. I feel that we have a lot of problems, that people have become so diverted by so many problems that they don't even have enough time to focus on them or find ways of getting out of them. Their perspectives have been blocked. . . . I think that is my basic role as a writer . . .

somebody has to speak and somebody has to change. I feel that history is made, not by accepting history as it is, but by people rewriting it. . . . I consider writing to be a dialogue between the writer and the society. . . . People create social conditions and people can change social conditions for the better."

In many ways, one might see Tess Onwueme as the Ibsen of her culture, the playwright who dares to raise new issues and write *A Doll's House*—so to speak—for her people. She is concerned, in her latest and most ambitious work, with themes that speak as much to men as women. Two such plays (not included in this book) address these topics.

"*Legacies* concerns an introspective search to rediscover black identity. It is based on black reconnaissance and the rebirth of our national conscience as a people. Set in a mythical Igbo kingdom called Idu, the play centers around a man and woman as symbols of Igbo familyhood. It signifies a return to African roots," the playwright explains. A Vice Chancellor's Command Performance of the play was held at Imo State University in 1989.

Like *The Desert Encroaches*, which won the Association of Nigerian Authors award in 1985, it is a departure from Onwueme's often feminine story line. Allegorical in style and universal in theme, *The Desert Encroaches* becomes symbolic of the ecological, moral, and socio-economic disaster upon us all, and takes a swipe at the propensity of people everywhere to hold conferences to worry about and study the situation while the politics of hunger, oppression, and total annihilation march on.

More recently a winner of the Martin Luther King Award for Distinguished Black Scholars, Onwueme has confirmed herself as a Nigerian writer of note, a glowing star in the firmament of dramatic art, an internationalist with universal themes for all. Reflected in the mirror of her Nigerian heritage, this playwright is to be read and enjoyed with the best contemporary drama has to offer. Her work demystifies the idea of theater as illusion, as something sacred, something we just offer for entertainment or emotional catharsis.

"I see theater as a group medium for dialogue in society. It shouldn't be that wall separating the audience from the actors on the stage. That fourth wall must be broken.

When you break that fourth wall, then there is participation. . . . It becomes a communal effort. Everybody becomes a part of it," says the playwright, who is a firm believer in Bertolt Brecht.

When one reads these plays, one feels a part of them, of the debate on stage, a debate for the entire populace of our Mother Earth, now more aware than ever of human rights issues everywhere, and now, more threatened than ever by their lack or demise. As the epilogue is chanted by the town crier at the end of *The Broken Calabash:* "The moon is full. The old season dies. A new crop is sown. What harvest do you foresee? Today is the climax of the festival ending the drudgery of the old season. The new yam will be eaten but it is streaked with blood. . . . And shall we eat the new yam with blood? Why must they turn our rite to tears?"

Daniella Gioseffi

New York City
1991

TESS ONWUEME'S SOULAR SYSTEM:

Trilogy of the She-Kings—Parables, Reigns, Calabashes

> "Anything which cannot stand the force of change must be uprooted or be blown into oblivion by the storm heralding the new season!"
>
> Ona, *The Broken Calabash*

> "The task of woman is to build—to create."
>
> Zo, *Parables for a Season*

> "How do you think
> You can snap the finger without the
> Right thumb?"
>
> Omu, *The Reign of Wazobia*

Does it widen our awe of Tess Onwueme's dramaturgical sorcery to know that, though still in her mid-thirties, she has "authored" five children, a Ph.D. in dramatic literature, more than sixteen plays (ten published), and scores of intergenerational hook-ups, lectures, cultural reunions, articles, choral/ritual performances, and poems? That her stunning plays, spun from the rich threads of West African culture, have enjoyed international premieres at the Bonstelle Theater in Detroit, the National Theatre of Nigeria, and the First International Conference on Women Playwrights in Buffalo, New York? Or that she was the first and only female to win the Drama Prize given by the Association of Nigerian Authors (in 1985, for *The Desert Encroaches*) and the first woman to act as president of the ANA? Perhaps . . . perhaps. What it does widen, however, is our appreciation of a life committed, a life experiential, a life dramatic, and a life prolific. These lives, stitched into the *kente* of righteous creativity, weave regal woman, familial/ancestral struggles, bidimensional sojourns, and truncated/reconstructed legacies (see *Legacies*, 1988) into joy- or pain-colored theatrical tapestries.

Certainly, *The Broken Calabash, Parables for a Season,* and *The Reign of Wazobia* may be seen on the one hand as a trilogy. But they also may be enjoyed as distinct and self-woven fabrics of drama, adhering to their own pattern-frames of time, logic, space, and rhythm yet threaded into an ancient-to-current continuum made whole and healthy by belief system, mythopoeic ritual, parable, humor, satire, proverb, ceremony, soul-tossing conflict, and folkadelic webbing. Of this dramaturge's important work, Kendall, chair of the Department of Theater at Smith College, has noted:

> Her plays not only bring the range and beauty of Nigerian culture to an international audience, they create the artistic bridges crucial to the development of a multicultural educational environment. In *Legacies,* for example, she explores the links and breakages between African-American and African peoples. In *The Reign of Wazobia,* she examines the intersections of tradition and ritual, the construction of gender, and the construction of "woman," in a framework which is particular to Nigeria but which is pertinent to women in the U.S.A. and many other countries. (correspondence, June 18, 1991)

Onwueme's cultural influences and aesthetic kinships may be said to span a good stretch of the Afrocentric, Eurocentric, and multicultural rainbow: oral literature and folklore, Elizabethan (especially Shakespeare) and modern European drama, African and black diasporan expression. Among her literary soul mates are Wole Soyinka, Ama Ata Aidoo, Samuel Beckett, Derek Walcott, John Pepper Clark, Albert Camus, Chinua Achebe, Toni Morrison, Anton Chekhov, Femi Osofisan, Ngugi Wa Thiong'O, George Bernard Shaw, Athol Fugard, August Wilson, Amos Tutuola, Gloria Naylor, Buchi Emecheta, Dennis Brutus, Alex LaGuma, Mariama Ba, and Sembene Ousmane.

Onwueme's plays, inside and outside this collection, transmit certain messages on both ostensible and figurative levels. *Levels* is a good word here, for upon entering On-wueme's dramatic "soular system," one is simultaneously engaged by numerous dimensions: feminine and feminist, tangible and ethereal, god and mortal, woman and man, she-king and he-queen, astral and physical, empowered and unempowered, democratic and fascistic, ancient and present, Afrocentric and Eurocentric. (One must hasten to add, however, that her work is never so contrived or fragmented that it can be reduced to predictable polarities and dualities.) Add this: "revolt of intellectual modernity against a decadent traditional value of the caste order" and "the individual conviction of insurmountability of genuine love for another person in spite of traditional and unholy attitudes of discrimination" (introductory notes to the first edition, *The Broken Calabash*).

But what, ostensibly, are these plays "about"? For starters, they "dramatically" suggest a rearrangement of the world so as to strip it of male hegemony, class oppression, indifference to youth, needless war ("When, when, when will men learn to accept that they cannot gain peace from war?" Wazobia, *The Reign of Wazobia*), blind deference to elders ("Longevity is no measure of wisdom," Wazobia, *Wazobia*), counterproductive power struggles (especially in *Parables for a Season* and *The Reign of Wazobia*), and the "leprous grip of the disease of freedom" (metaphor for "whitebody"—Igbo euphemism for leprosy—and the oxymoronic role of white missionaries).

But the "about" factor has a flip side to it: herein the same images, folk webbings, faith structures, poetic testimonials, ceremonies, combative dialogues, and sermonical soliloquies are employed, not in stripping a world (*soular system?*), but in rituals of cultural coherence, reclamation, rescue, and reconstruction. Within this context of therapeutic remythification, the She-King Trilogy (as I call it) is about the healing salve of humor, as in signifying ("feet so long they can stand on the moon," Zo, *Wazobia*); the intrinsic value of women to men and women to women ("With or without man, make a meaning of your life," Wazobia, *Wazobia*); the predominance of the proverb in African cultures as an educational tool ("A child who asks questions never misses the road," Priest of Ani, *Wazobia*); the need for cross-gender collaboration and harmony: the a priori view of mother as Earth/Earth as mother ("Mother, you are deep like the Earth herself," Zo, *Parables for a Season*); the culturally centered position of the black male child and the ominous historical threat to his survival ("Ah—world! / A black male child costly as a gem / And I who longed for one since I / lost my twins to the slave raiders, to / be blessed with a male child . . . ?" Old Termite, *Parables*); and irrevocable ties to past and land ("umbilical cords were buried right at the root of trees in this very soil," Wazobia, *Wazobia*).

In this young playwright's mind's eye, African theater, the oldest in the world, burns full up with folk- and funk-spun energy, rich and robust giggle-humor, raw visceral movement, acrobatic intelligence, life-death intimacies ("We live in the twin-fold of life and death," Wazobia, *Parables*), pageantry, town criers, griots, gods ("Sometimes the gods like to humor us in our shame," Idehen, *Wazobia*), masks and masking ("We all wear more than one face at a time in this society," Ona, *Calabash*), conflict, ritual dancers, contradictions waiting to be satirized ("You Christians and your lord who forbids stealing and yet calls himself a thief (in the night)," Courtuma, *Calabash*), music, poetry, fetishes, shrines, body decorations, and festivals.

Onwueme has meticulously and brilliantly restitched many of these traditional and modern elements into plays that are temporally cyclical, thematically modal, ideo-rhythmically intricate, and histrionically edifying. In these woman- and god-centered tapestries and murals, Onwueme's workswomanship, reminiscent of sister-scholar-artists like Zora Neale Hurston and Katherine Dunham, is revealed as consummate and whole. Like her foremothers (and forefathers), she probes the deep ancient underpinnings of culture, character, image conduit, and ritual. Such probings have taken her into the multidimensional worlds of myth breaking, mythmaking, and myth merging. As an African-Nigerian-Igbo-woman-feminist-artist, Onwueme in her life and history has been, at least on one level, configured by colonialism, tribalism, imperialism, racism, sexism, stereotype, and classism. In *The Broken Calabash, The Reign of Wazobia,* and *Parables for a Season,* she reimages, reforges, reshapes, resews, and reinvents woman/human societies for the stage.

The women in this trilogy are all ascending. Involved women. Evolved women. Evolving women. African women

with themselves, their men, their children, their families,
their neighbors. Extended families. Black folks. Though
there are forces that would devolve—and, if possible, dissolve—them. Through drama (life-mirroring), Onwueme lifts
these women, helps them—and their men—resee and receive themselves as ancient, traditional, and reenvisioned
citizens. Woman as king; man as cohort; the sin of too much
father-love—a tragic, stifling love—for daughter in *Calabash*;
king-mother roles in Aniocha-Igbo society; the clash of historical myth and revolutionary-intellectual modernity; re-
adapting precolonial mother-daughter relationships to
contemporary needs and values; harmonizing African inde-
pendence, pan-Africanism, and Afrocentricity with cross-
cultural black consciousness (again, see *Legacies*). Such
are the major themes and major schemes of Onwueme
as she manipulates vision, canvas, stage, village, festival,
campus, chorus, sitting room, masquerade, symbol, sign,
etymology, anthropology, ethnography, mythology, xylophone, gong, *ekwe, kente,* high life, music, birth, death,
and marriage. Hers is a multicultural theatrical spectrum
that encompasses the Afro-Indian-Greco-Roman-Hebrew-
Christian-European continuum.

In *Parables for a Season* and *The Reign of Wazobia*
women who by law or tradition have rightfully ascended to
the kingship—even if only temporarily—are being under-
mined by men, occasionally by women, and sometimes in
the context of cross-gender plotting. One of the male strate-
gies is all too familiar to African-American villagers: the
divide-and-conquer pattern. Iyase, who plots with Idehen
(Iago?) against newly crowned she-king Wazobia, notes:

> We must catch the lion by getting hold of its cub. In
> spite of avowed solidarity, women are women. You can-
> not rule out petty jealousies among them.
> Throw a grain of maize on a brood of chicks. Grip the
> hen as they cackle for the booty. (*Wazobia*)

But as the plot and plotting thicken, as the "men hold their
meeting to unseat Wazobia," the wise elder stateswoman
Omu directs the women thusly:

> Together we form this moon shape. Lie in ambush sur-
> rounding the throne as the men emerge. We, together

in this naked legion, will salute them in our natural state. Taunting their eyes with their own shame. This naked dance is a last resort women have had over the ages. If our men force us to the wall, we must use it as our final weapon. Unusual problems demand unusual solutions. (*Wazobia*)

In Onwueme's soular system, women cannot be reduced to a group of quarreling chicks. Instead, they induce and sustain bonding, express solidarity, and when tempers flare and there is a call for vengeful violence, Wazobia reminds them of their mission: "Women peace! Peace! Spill no blood! Ours is to plant seed-yams. Not blood to feed worms." This young king/queen knows that the song (the word, *nommo,* songified naming) is the *thing.* Traditionally, one exorcises ugliness and expiates evil and bad feelings through the use of song and *callings* (as in blues). So Wazobia steadies her sisters (and us) with this war-peace cry:
"Sing, women! Stand firm on the soil! Sing! Sing!

Eugene B. Redmond

East St. Louis
Summer 1991

The
Broken
Calabash

CAST

This version of *The Broken Calabash* was first produced at the National Theater Iganmu, Lagos, from October 26–28, 1984, with the following cast:

ONA (JEWEL): *Second-year student in a local university (Lizzy Ucheagauwa)*

UGO: *Ona's friend and classmate (Beatrice Oguike)*

COURTUMA, CHIEF ELOKE RAPU: *Ona's father, about 55 years old, once a court messenger (Mike Iheadindu)*

OLIAKU RAPU: *Ona's mother (Grace Ayozie)*

DIAKU: *Ona's fiancé, a youth corps member (Ewa Okechukwu Ogbonnia)*

OTU AGADA: *Diaku's father (Sam Ihenagwam)*

TOWN CRIER: *(Ambrose Agomuo)*

DIBIA: *Village priest (Ambrose Agomuo)*

JESTER: *(Christopher Oguzie)*

VILLAGE WOMEN: *(Kate Uchewuakor and Loveline Iroakazi)*

VILLAGE GIRLS: *(Christy Njoku, Christy Ukaegbu, Celine Ebom)*

MAIDENS: *(Kate Ogbonna, Rose Ben Orji, Lizzy Odom, Loveline Iroakazi, Adline Elezianya)*

EKETE: *Courtuma's kinsman (Stephen Yisa Daniel)*

ADAGOR: *Courtuma's younger sister (Christiana Ukaegbu)*

SATIRICAL DANCERS: *(Erege Ngozi, Stephen Ukaegbu, Innocent Mbonu, Iweha Onyena, Christopher Oquzie, Julius Obiefunne, Tunji Akintayo)*

PROLOGUE

The scene is a village square. Enter TOWN CRIER *with a gong.*

TOWN CRIER:
Kom! Kom! Kom!
Ogwashi ebo iteeni.
The sun has passed the center of the head.
Leaves are browning.
The barns ready to be laden and plaited.
And the season's fowls ready to roost.
Has the homestead been swept for the yam spirit?
Will all waists swing at Ine festival?
Will all lips smile at Ine festival?
Will all mouths taste the new yam?
This is the message. I am only the bearer—O!
Kom! Kom! Kom!
(*As* TOWN CRIER *announces, a group of village maidens on their way to the stream begins to assemble to listen to the announcement and soon breaks into a song.* ONA, COURTUMA, *and* OLIAKU *come to peep at the singers who beckon on* ONA *to come and join them.* COURTUMA *waves at* ONA *to return to their house while he and* OLIAKU *continue watching.* OLIAKU *throws nzu or native white chalk in their direction and disappears with* COURTUMA *while* UGO *passes by the singers to join* ONA.)

22

MAIDENS' SONG

Ọkọ–Ọkọ–lọ–K–ọ–ọ–ọ
Ọkpa kwa nuo
ewooo
Ọkpa kwaooo
Kanyi je iyi o o o *(two times)*
Kanyi je iyi o o o neneee–o
Ọkpa akwana akwana
N'ọkpa akwa gaa lio o o
Anyi ge je ọzọ ooo
Eh iya a e e e
Nwabuzọ bia o o o

Kanyi jee–o o o
Otegee isi bume mbumo
Na ntutu akwacha sia lio
akwali lia elue nmọ–o o o
Eheee iya eheee
Ona Nwa Rapu weli ndidi–o o o
Kanyi–jee–o o o
Ofuonye amasi ije no odudu atagbue nueo
Ogo go goo
goo gooo, eei iyaaa, eeee. Ona Nwa Rapu
bia–o
Kanyi jeee

(Chorus:)
Kanyi ejiyi
Kanyi etiwe
Kanyi elu no
Kanyi akwama
Anyi ge je ọzọ
eh iyaa
eh,
Nwabuzọ
Kanyi jeeeo

TRANSLATION OF THE SONG:

The cock crows
Oko ko lo ko o o
Alas, the cock has crowed.
The cock has crowed

> Let us go to the stream *(twice)*
> Let us go to the stream Nene
> Mr. Cock, do not crow
> Cock do not crow *(two times)*
>
> Cock do not crow
> but it has already crowed
> We must go again
> Alas, we must go again
> Our leader, come let us go

It is long since the head started carrying calabashes. The head must be getting bald. Alas, this melancholic song must be reaching the ancestors, Nwabuzo. Come, let us depart. It isn't proper for one person alone to set out on a journey.

> Otherwise tse-tse flies will suck
> her dry and dead
> Ogo go go go o o o
> e e e i yaa e e e
> Nwabuzo come, let us go again.

MOVEMENT ONE

Midmorning in Isah Village. COURTUMA's *sitting room. Fairly modern but old headmaster-like furniture. Left side of the wall has picture of crucifix; on right side of wall hang red and white pieces of cloth with feathers. This looks like a family shrine.*

It is the end of November, about the end of a long vacation and the beginning of harvest which is preceded by the Ine satirical festival. ONA *sits alone listening to a blues tune from a cassette player. She appears to be totally entranced by the words and rhythm of this music. She follows the musician's heart and voice right from the beginning to the end, and as soon as the cassette claps to a halt, she unwinds herself, trying to refill the mysterious tape. A few minutes later, the tape signifies its readiness to communicate with her again. This time,* ONA *is not simply absorbed with her listening to the sound, but her voice competes with the artist's. She sings and dances to the tune. Suddenly, a compulsive knock at the door, and* UGO *storms in, swinging the door open.* ONA *starts and, too surprised to speak, remains glued to the floor.*

UGO:

Hmmm, my dear Ona, you must be enjoying yourself. To be singing and dancing and playing your music in these hard austerity times. Your star must be hotter than the sun. Or perhaps you have passed all your exams.

ONA:

So you think and are made to feel. But in actual fact, it's all a make-believe—mere photo trick which is a necessary insurance (or antidote?) for self-survival and self-realization in a world with neither worth nor direction. We all wear more than one face at a time in this society.

UGO:

World with neither worth nor direction? You must be joking, Ona. You must be joking. Or you're going crazy.

ONA:

Am I really? Perhaps I am.

UGO:

Of course, you are. Otherwise, how could you of all people be talking about the worthlessness of life? You, who are the salt of this place?

ONA: *(shrugging her shoulders)*

Me? Salt of this place? Oh bitterness! Then we'll all be invalidated when all the sweetness in us all is completely absorbed by this stagnant air of tradition.

UGO:

I don't understand what you mean.

ONA:

You are not expected to.

UGO:

But who are those expected to know?

ONA:

Those *directly* flowing with the new current which the wind of the old insists on drowning.

UGO:

I see . . .

ONA:

You don't see anything.

UGO:

Then we shall see *(sitting down;* ONA *does the same)*

ONA:

We may never live to witness it.

UGO:

That's if you don't wish to.

ONA:

Even if I did, what control do I exercise over anything?

UGO:

Perhaps the problem arises from your lack of self-assertion.

ONA:

Even if that means drowning in the wave to combat this inertia?

UGO:

There is no harm in trial.

ONA:

There is, I can assure you.

UGO:

Look, I've never had it so good, Ona. I wish that all these lecturers would continue their strike so that we'll go on perpetual holiday! I love being a student, Ona—the aura of university scholarship in Nigeria. The hairs stand to acclaim—even the elders offer you their seats once they hear you're the son of so-and-so in a university. You may even earn a standing ovation just for mentioning you're a Nigerian student studying abroad . . .

ONA: *(They shake hands)*

Come on!

UGO:

I wish I could be enrolled a perpetual student . . .

ONA:

Yes, people bow to you not because you're a student but because of the great potential they see in you—the potent power of potential—to command the ministries and houses of assemblies. To hold in your thumb the key to the nation's treasury—it's automatic not just with university education, but with money.

UGO:

And if you're expensively dressed, then you've captured them. At times the magic is done by wearing a T-shirt bearing the name of any university. It doesn't matter if that shirt was given to you as dash.

ONA:

Anyway, Ugo, all these don't really bother me right now. I have more fundamental issues that burn me presently.

UGO:

You mean it doesn't bother you that our values are so shallow?

ONA:

That is luxury! It is only people like you who enjoy such leisure—the luxury of freedom. As confining as the walls of the hostels are, I always feel freer on campus than in my own home. Isn't that ironic?

UGO:

Ona, please don't pull my legs. Who enjoys better home care and comfort than you? On campus, you seek attention, but at home, being an only child, all attention and tender loving care are lavished on you. Just you . . .

ONA:

And that's my undoing: my misery. I receive more than my fair share of love. I feel smothered. Just to go out like you now, I can't without a barrage of questions: Where are you going, Ona? Whom are you going to? Why must you go now? Etc. etc. Most times, to avoid conflict and embarrassment, I stay put in the house. My father especially, he loves me too much. I'm hardly on good terms with my mother. But my father—he can go any length with me. My father will do anything to keep me and make me happy.

UGO:

He must be possessive.

ONA:

Not possessive. But his kind of love is consuming. I even doubt if he ever showed any woman, including my mother, half as much love as he's showing and giving me. It's an embarrassing type of love. I wish he loved me less.

UGO:

And I wish mine loved me more. Isn't it an irony of life?

ONA:

Yes, indeed—an accident of birth. I wish I had a choice when I was coming.

UGO:

Well, I wouldn't really be that pessimistic if I were you. After all, it's only a temporary problem—just when you come on holidays. On campus, you can maximize your activities, spread your tentacles since they'll soon be pruned at home. It's easy. Just pretend like everybody else, that all is well.

ONA:

Ugo, it's not as easy as you think. Can you foresee me leaving this home for marriage?

UGO:

Of course, yes! Of course, yes! That'll solve all your problems.

ONA:

Or highlight it, you mean?

UGO:

How can? All your problems will evaporate the moment you show him a fiancé. He'll then understand that you're no longer his helpless, loving baby, but his hopeful loving daughter. He can't keep you in the house forever! Neither can he marry you!

ONA:

If it were possible, he would. . . . I just wish all this would end soon.

UGO:

For you to form a new life?

ONA:

Above all, to see life in its fullness. Not so early, though. When you've seen it so early, there's no more aspiration, and it tapers off. Better to go slowly, meet the knots, and untie them gradually until the cycle is complete.

ONA:

Not in everything, though. *(They eye each other and chuckle)*

UGO:

Yes, I know when you want a fast and rapid motion—when DK is around. I envy you. Anybody would want a rapid motion with Diaku—Diaku. How is he, by the way?

ONA:

He's fine.

UGO:

Have you seen him since last Sunday?

ONA:

No, but he promised to come today.

UGO:

No wonder your blood is boiling today. I don't blame you.

ONA:

It's more distressing for one to feel and not express one-self. My father inhibits me in every way. He always hangs around whenever Diaku comes to see me. Since my father only permits me to attend service on Sundays, Diaku and I have devised a means of beating time. I normally look forward to Sundays when Diaku and I can both elope from the church after the gospel to his house. And as soon as we guess the service is over, I wipe my lips and fly home as if no sugar can dissolve in my mouth.

UGO:

Hmm. Let them meet you and Diaku, then they'll know that sugar won't only melt but burn, too. These parents think they're very clever.

ONA:

And insist on roping their experiences around you.

UGO:

So it's a battle of wits. Often, they are the losers.

ONA:

So it may seem in the long run. Just in the long run, but I have one fear.

UGO: *(concerned)*

What else can be your fear, that Diaku would be snatched from you by another girl? (ONA *gives* UGO *a pat on the face)*

ONA:

Well, that's not impossible with these handsome young men of nowadays.

UGO:

And the adventurous and hyperactive young women . . . What's your fear, anyway?

ONA:

I have been dreaming of snails lately.

UGO:

Snails? Is that all? It's only snails?

ONA:

Yes, snails . . .

UGO:

And you allow that to bother you? This old man must be feeding a lot of superstition into your head, you know.

ONA:

No, Ugo. I have always known, and my mother also tells me that snails are evil—*Uke*. Snail signifies sacrifice.

UGO:

That's if you believe in it. And perhaps you think about it, hence you dream recurrently about it.

ONA:

Let's check in my zoological dictionary. *(goes to fetch the dictionary, returns shortly with it, both read out)* "Snail, of the mollusk family with shell, soft body, no limbs. Hermaphrodite."

ONA:

Hmm. Hermaphrodite? You see the meaning?

UGO:

It's of no consequence, is it? A mere harmless and peace-loving animal. Not even risking conflict with a lover. I shouldn't mind that if I were you. *(UGO rises up to leave)*

ONA:

Thanks a lot for your valuable company. My association with you has always been a source of enlightenment. Our relationship has always given me cause for excitement.

UGO: *(now at the door)*

'Bye, Ona. It's been a day.

ONA:

'Bye, and thank you.

(As ONA is seeing off UGO, they are met by SATIRICAL DANC-ERS *celebrating the Ine festival. The mock dancers taunt them to the extent that UGO pushes one of them down. Exit dancers)*

UGO:

Who are those street urchins?

ONA:

They're my people. They're celebrating the Ine festival.

UGO:
  Hmm. Is that how you people do it here?
ONA:
  Yes, funny, isn't it?
UGO:
  Na wa yaoo! See you anyway.
ONA:
  'Bye, 'bye.
  (Exeunt, lights out)

MOVEMENT TWO

COURTUMA, *making a climbing rope in his Ogwa; enter his kinsman,* EKETE.

EKETE:
  Diokpa Rapu, Ụwa Ọma-o.
COURTUMA: *(offering him a seat)*
  Ụwa Ọma nwam
ADAGOR: *(entering from another direction; her voice is heard before she is seen)*
  Ụwa Ọ ma-o
COURTUMA:
  O nwam
  Ụnụ apụta gọ ụla?
ADAGOR:
  Eeinna nna-anyi. Ona kwanu?
COURTUMA: *(scratches his head, calling)*
  Ona! O Ona!
ONA: *(entering)*
  Yes, Papa! *(She notices* ADAGOR *and embraces her;* ADA-GOR, *happy to see her, looks intently at* ONA; *in fact, she surveys* ONA*)*
ADAGOR: *(hand on cheek, shakes her head slowly)*
  Ona, Ona, the star in the middle of the night, the one piece of yam that reaches the whole world. *(Turning to* COURTUMA*)* Nnanyi, now the hen is cackling, it is time to

keep it to roost, so it doesn't drop the eggs on stone. Will Ona get her wife this holiday? And at this time of Ine, girls abound . . .

(She senses that no one is replying to her, begins to check herself—too late. While she is saying this, ONA slowly disengages herself from ADAGOR's embrace and stares at her, mouth agape. The outstretched hands are frozen as she slowly begins to retreat into the house, COURTUMA subdued, EKETE cupping his mouth)

COURTUMA:
Adagor . . . Adagor . . . Adagor!

ADAGOR:
Nnanyi, I'm here.

COURTUMA:
Remember that a tse-tse fly perched on the scrotum must be chased away with extreme care . . .

EKETE: *(shaking his head in resignation)*
Hmm, hmm. *(turning to ADAGOR)* You, woman, with tongue as sharp as the edge of a cutlass. Don't you know that the itch in the eye must be scratched with extreme caution? *(ADAGOR looks on, aghast)*

COURTUMA:
Softly, softly lest the egg breaks in the delivery . . .
(He looks intently at the ground for some time, scratches his leg with cutlass in his hand, blows his nose, and rubs it on his ankle.)

EKETE: *(beckoning on ADAGOR, who obeys him)*
Nnanyi, Rapu. We are coming. *(COURTUMA still lost in thought when OLIAKU enters)*

OLIAKU: *(gleefully)*
Today, my dear lord, we must count our blessings for his kindness in giving us this one child. Could you have imagined life without her?

COURTUMA:
Oliaku, thank God for our singular fortune. No seer could have convinced me that we would still be married today but for our Jewel.

OLIAKU: *(turning to the shrine in the courtyard)*
All the herbs, drugs, and medicines I drank in this world, just to have her? *(She kneels down in supplication, arms outstretched to God)* God, may your name be forever

praised. Me, the mother of a child in the "unifersity"? God be praised. My fathers know that their names must not be lost to history.

COURTUMA:

Well, let's not be overjoyed yet. Our people say that if dusk doesn't come, one cannot criticize the day.

OLIAKU:

Even if it ends here, it is still cause for joy.

COURTUMA:

Be careful, for tomorrow is pregnant. None knows what it will give birth to.

OLIAKU:

You remember the Dibia's pronouncement before my Ona was conceived? That the goddess of the sea, Onokwu, has corked all their children and not mine in a bottle. And for this reason, it was futile attempting to have a child against the goddess's will.

COURTUMA:

Then he said that if we insisted, he could intercede for us to the goddess, knowing that she would yield to our request. Yet he warned that we were best for not having one, for a sheep with only a ram as child is really childless, and such a child would complicate our lives.

OLIAKU:

Well, the complication is what we are seeing today. Our Jewel in a "unifersity". She will be our mouth, our eyes, our ears, both here at home and beyond the seas.

COURTUMA:

It's good to sit back and narrate all these to the listening ear. In those days the muscles of my face were too tight to spread even for a smile. What with the constant taunting and insinuations by in-laws and neighbors who bred them like sheep. And we even allowed ourselves to be converted to Christianity. Afumata—o! Yesterday has become history. *(He walks up to the crucifix and turns its face down. And as if timed, the church bell is heard at that moment.* COURTUMA, *startled, listens for a while and ignores it)*

OLIAKU:

Indeed, it is the gods that chase away flies that pester a tail-less cow. Obida nwa ngene, I thank you.

COURTUMA:

Now that Ona is on holidays, you must begin to introduce the topic to her slowly.

OLIAKU:

Which topic?

COURTUMA:

You surprise me, you know? Each time I discuss with you, you talk like a person while we're still together, but once I turn my back, your brain turns into a basket and empties all its contents. If your tongue is too heavy to speak the white man's language, is there a hole also pierced in your brain to empty all its contents?

OLIAKU:

Hmm, call me what you like. My problem is that I'm overwhelmed by my luck.

COURTUMA:

Enough of that now lest we count our chicks before they're hatched. Now, seriously, you must from now try to impress it upon Ona that she must begin to have in mind the wife we must marry for her.

OLIAKU:

Oh! Is that what you were referring to? You should have pronounced it outright, because there's nothing secret about it. Everyone from Aniocha, not to talk of Ogwashi-uku, knows that a girl as only child must either be kept at home as Idegbe to bear children for her father or marry a wife to propagate that line.

COURTUMA:

Hmm, Oliaku. We must be cautious. Life is no longer as simple as that. Times are changing, and we must not pretend as if the harmattan wind cannot char our skin, too. Ona has acquired the white man's knowledge and wisdom which is good for us in many respects. But at times, our customs are too entrenched, too old to bend or be married to the new ways. What we achieve by sending Ona to school at all is to make up in terms of our lack of number. That we may not die wanting and longing to enter a car owned by other people's children, who know and who can tap the tree of the white man's wealth.

OLIAKU:

Also that she may read and interpret my letters from my relatives in Lagos who have gone to do the white man's job and have "lost their language" in the process. Why must our own relatives write to me in a foreign language they know I neither speak nor understand? I know I'm illiterate. But I also know what I'm talking about. Why must my own sisters write to me in a language I cannot understand?

COURTUMA:

That is not the point, anyway. The point is that even if they write to you in Igbo, can you read it? Then forget it and think of the issue of my Ona. You must treat the topic with caution, or else we will antagonize her, especially since her mates can influence her. I have seen a glimpse of the white man's rays and how powerful they can be—all that while I was the court messenger!

OLIAKU:

Why don't you introduce the topic to her yourself? You're more tactful with such delicate matters than I am. Moreover, your word to Ona is gospel. *(As she's saying this,* ONA'*s footstep is heard outside. They listen and watch* ONA *walk in to them)*

ONA:

Papa, I've come to announce to you that I'm going out.

COURTUMA:

Where to? And with your hair scattered like Oyiliya, the husk of a palm fruit bunch? No, my dear, you can't.

ONA:

Papa, but, there's nothing wrong with my hair. It is the hairstyle in vogue—waves, they call it.

OLIAKU:

Waves! Let the wind be blowing you two there. I must go and cook so that waves don't carry us all away like feathers. *(Sensing an argument about to ensue,* OLIAKU *slips away)*

ONA:

Papa, but I thought you liked modernization.

COURTUMA:

Yes, I do. But not when you fry your hair to look like a rat that has fallen into oil. The beauty of plaited hair is indisputable to any man with nerves and veins inside him.

ONA:

Plaiting my hair? I can't remember when I last did that. It is obsolete! To plait my hair and look like an Ekpo mask?

No! What we need is to disentangle some of the areas that make things too rigid and unmanageable. We must apply heat or relaxer to straighten them in our days.

COURTUMA:

By the time your hair becomes straight, we would have long been gone. *(COURTUMA pensive, as if dreading the idea of death)*

ONA:

But at least you would have seen the beginning of the drama before your departure.

COURTUMA:

That's left to you, the modern, to execute. Where did you say you were going? *(sound of church bell interrupting the conversation)*

ONA:

To confession . . .

COURTUMA:

Confession? What for? What is your sin? The sin of not going to confession last week. You are incapable of sinning, my Jewel. Forget it. There is nothing like that where you are. Don't allow all these so-called priests who wear long gowns like women to bog you down with weights of rules and irrelevant doctrines.

ONA:

Papa, you must let me go. Otherwise, I can't receive holy communion on Sunday.

COURTUMA:

That is better. Don't let it bother you. I brew the best palm wine in Isah, and we can buy biscuits, too. Time was when I did that because we wanted a child. White man's communion? *(spits with disgust)* I have seen the cassock, my dear child, and I can show you that what that priest has in them I have, too. If he, another man, can forgive your sin and hold you captive with his biscuits and wine, what wonders would the power of juice from—from a loving father not do?

ONA:

That could be dangerous!

COURTUMA:

Not when it is a natural expression from a father's bosom to a loving child like you? *(OLIAKU comes in)*

OLIAKU: *(trying to lighten the tension)*
So you two lovers are still at your talk?

COURTUMA:

No, we were simply joking. The matter is over. I can't let my Jewel *(giving* ONA *a pat on the shoulder)* go yet. She must wait until I have discharged . . . *(They all stop to listen to the* TOWN CRIER, *whose voice can be heard from the village square. He is now within sight of the audience. The* TOWN CRIER *beats his gong three times, each time before he makes his announcement)*

TOWN CRIER:

Isah! The Ine to purge the land of evil of the old year is at hand. Our hope lies in you, the youth. Therefore, you must heartily satirize those sons and daughters of iniquity who, year in, year out, pollute our land by their ways and deeds. This is the time for weeding. The stage has been set in motion. Anyone singled out as the polluter of our land must pay the final debt to the gods. Only if the gods are pleased can we then eat the new yam, after this season.

This is the message. *Kom!*
This is what I have been instructed to tell you. *Kom!*

A message does not kill its bearer—o. *(Exit* TOWN CRIER; *leaves* OLIAKU *and* COURTUMA *groping for words)*

COURTUMA:

Hmm, yes, Ona, as I was saying, you cannot go today. *(*ONA *leaves for her room, sulking.* OLIAKU *and* COURTUMA *become fidgety, looking each other in the face.* COURTUMA *is most hurt. Soon he begins to pace about the room, then disappears toward* ONA's *bedroom. As* TOWN CRIER *is leaving, ·he is followed by a comic/satirical scene of mock dancers. First, a group of young men and boys, dressed in brassieres, wigs, lipstick, rags, skirts, ladies' clothes, and high-heeled shoes, dances across the square. Soon after, girls dressed in men's clothes, beards, one-eyed goggles, etc., chant songs and dance. They all chant songs against people who have transgressed the customs of the land. When they meet the boys, both groups coo and boo each other, with the boys chasing the girls from the square)*

MOCK SONG BY GIRLS

Nene Akwazia

Nene akwazi—o
Nene akwazie kamgbanite—o
Baba akwazie—o
Baba akwazie kamgbanite
Kamgbanite nige enwe ego
N'ofu mgbala otaba
N'ofu mgbala otaba emee
Nnu ego

TRANSLATION OF THE SONG

Leader: Mama, do not cry
Chorus: Mama, do not cry, let me grow up
Leader: Papa, do not cry
Chorus: Papa, do not cry, let me grow up
Leader: Let me grow up
Chorus: Let me grow up
Leader: For one line of tobacco
Chorus: One line of tobacco now costs a mil-
          lion naira

(ONA *alone in her room. To ease tension, she begins to hum another blues tune.* COURTUMA *interrupting and approaching to hang his arms around her neck)*

COURTUMA:

Don't be weary, my child. You can't fathom the extent of my love for you. Don't look with such unkind eyes at your darling father. I am still the Rapu, the one and only papa you've always toddled toward. *(trying to be funny)* Or is the university promising you a new father, a godfather? Eh? Don't worry, my own Jewel. My eye, my mouth. Don't you know you mean more than daughter to me? *(ONA getting embarrassed, pushes him gently away)*

ONA:

Papa, you've again started with these your superlatives with which you entrap me—

COURTUMA: *(upset)*

Entrap you? No, my Ona. Never use such terms again *(calming down again)* No, my little salt that gives taste to the soup. My little dry meat that fills the mouth. My speck of Jewel that outshines strings and strings of metal others use as ornaments. My diamond. Hmmm. It is I, your father, Eloke Jide Ọnwọ Rapu, son of Awaliégo, people who measure money with baskets. I, who am your father and will always be father of your children generation after generation, even from my grave! You are my savior, my comforter. *(OLIAKU's voice can be heard)*

OLIAKU:
My lord, are you all still there? Is our Jewel all right?

COURTUMA:
Yes. You know I have a magic wand with my Jewel.

OLIAKU:
Come, my lord, your food must be getting cold.

COURTUMA:
Nothing is as sweet as my girl, Oliaku.

OLIAKU:
Come now, your sweet one must sleep her afternoon sleep. *(Exit* COURTUMA *and* OLIAKU. ONA *alone)*

ONA:
Each time this fire wells up in my mind, he comes to pour cold water on it with his words, his touch. It is good for me to have such a dedicated father. I wish God gives me a husband like him, my father . . .

(revolting) But must all my life revolve around him so? So circumscribed by him? Must I never live my life independent of him? Must he always leave his mark on me? At school, it is father. At home, father. At play? Fa—Why can't I be independent? Oh, my father, how I love you and cherish you. But why must you tear me away from myself? Or is that a penalty for loving you?
(Knock at the door. ONA *reluctantly rises, peeps through the window to see the face of the intruder, sees it and beckons. Rushes to the door immediately to usher in* UGO. UGO *looks gorgeous).*

Hmmm. Ugo, how sweet you look. You must be up to some mischief.

UGO: *(strutting about)*
Well, mischief moves the world. I am going for disco. Live band! Eric Akaeze entertaining tonight—TDB. Are you coming, or will your father tie you down again?

ONA:

You know he will use his ropes on me.

UGO:

Hmm. You and this your father self. Is he your lover that he must have such hold on you? Anyway, you give him the encouragement.

ONA:

But, Ugo, you know my position, my situation within this family.

UGO:

Okay—o o o, na you sabi, stay and freak with your father. I'll go funky with my sugar daddy, too.

ONA:

Don't be silly, Ugo. You mean to tell me you're no longer with Chuks?

UGO:

Okay—o! Dey there sit-don-look. Life needs change—and the world goes round. See that wall clock. Is it static? No! Then we must move on. Variety is not just the spice but the real condiment of life.

(As UGO *talks,* ONA *observes with astonishment)* Hmm, don't look so shocked. Life must go on. Who would have thought the way I loved Chuks that I'd ever find fault with him? Today, I can. The Earth is not static, you know? You remember the theory of motion? We must move on. After all, people say that one cannot watch a dance only from one spot. Hmm—life. The way I feel now? Love—love is just nothing but pain, pain, pain with a bit of joy. That's all. Are you going or not?

ONA:

My father . . . My father . . .

UGO:

Do I go then?

ONA:

No, I must go today. But let's tell my father that we're going for catechism in preparation for confirmation. *(COUR-TUMA at that very moment is passing through the parlor and overhears* ONA *mentioning catechism and confirmation, although he doesn't know what it is all about)*

COURTUMA: *(entering the room)*

Confession, catechism, confirmation. "Con" this, "con" that. The white man and his priests have nothing else to offer us but "cons" *(He is now well inside the room. He finds* UGO *and* ONA. *Stops to answer* UGO's *greeting)*

UGO:
Good afternoon, sir. Good afternoon, sir!

COURTUMA: *(coldly)*
Afu-ta-no! So it's you who have come to see Ona?

ONA: *(displeased with the reception)*
Papa, it's my bosom friend, Ugo. You've met her here several times, or have you forgotten her?

COURTUMA: *(still cold)*
No! Is she not Ogbe's daughter from Azungwu?

ONA and UGO:
Yes, she is.

COURTUMA:
Hmm, you're welcome. But Ona, let me see you as soon as she leaves. I must talk to you.

ONA:
But, Papa, that will be after my return from catechism. Ugo and I are going to church. We're among those to be confirmed next time the bishop comes.

COURTUMA:
It is irrelevant: white man's confession and confirmation. A vicious circle. At catechism they teach you that your baptism is incomplete without confirmation. My question is, if their baptismal water is that potent, why must they need all the confirmation and a million sacraments to confirm the baptism? Sacrament of birth, sacrament of food, sacrament of drink, sacrament of death—all the nations of sakaras and praying mantis. No, my child, you must see through these people as I have. Leave their ways. It's distracting.
*(*COURTUMA *turning to* UGO*)* But you, how do you want to enter the church with your hair open, your back bare, and your lips as red as ulcer? That priest is human, you know? I can bet you that the catechist will wait until mass is far gone, and then he will send you out of the church for indecent dressing. You girls of nowadays must be taught to dress properly.
*(*ONA *is thoroughly embarrassed.* UGO *attempts to leave)*

ONA: *(holding* UGO *back)*
Father!

UGO:

Leave me.

ONA:

Please, Ugo!

UGO:

Let me go!

COURTUMA:

Leave her. Ona, let her go. Why must she come dressed like that to my house? Does she think this is a whorehouse? (UGO *is now outside the door*)

UGO:

Shit!

ONA:

Father! Oh, father . . . (*Silence, then a few minutes later,* COURTUMA *disappears.* ONA *throws herself down into a chair. Sound of gong again*)

TOWN CRIER:

Isha!

I must warn you again. *Kom!*

The grounds are cleared. *Kom!*

Be on your guard against mischief. *Kom!*

We are in a period of transition. *Kom!*

New yam must be eaten. *Kom!*

The leaves are turning yellow. *Kom!*

Beetles must be crushed. *Kom!*

It is the message. *Kom!*

I am only the bearer—o! *Kom!*

(*Slow fade-out of light*)

MOVEMENT THREE

Night. DIAKU *in* ONA*'s house. Fresh flowers on the table.* ONA*'s door is ajar.* COURTUMA *in the sitting room almost as a watchdog to the couple. On the table, there is candlelight being swayed by the wind. From time to time,* COURTUMA *pulls the curtain to make sure he sees what goes on between* ONA *and* DIAKU*.* ONA *and* DIAKU *pretend to be reading the Bible,* DIAKU*'s hand under* ONA*'s thigh.*

DIAKU: *(very relaxed)*
Big Papa, you are never tired staying up so late after the day's hard work on the farm?

COURTUMA:
Not when I still have this much life in me and when wolves pry around my chicks. *(COURTUMA continues snuffing and rubbing his thumb on his right leg as he snuffs and sneezes)*

DIAKU:
Oh, yeah? Great Papa! Ona, is there anywhere one can buy drink for the old folk to warm up?

ONA: *(rising)*
Yes.

COURTUMA:
Go to where, Ona?

ONA and DIAKU:
To buy drinks for you.

COURTUMA:
I need no such drink now. I must see clearly with my eyes. The only request I wish to make, however, is that you, Diaku, son of Otu Agada, must sit upright and not lean on the wall. *(DIAKU and ONA whisper)* Or do your people sit with their back and not their bottom? Secondly, you must continue talking, both of you. And lastly, make sure you don't shade that candlelight. I want to see everything clearly.

ONA:
Papa, but the heat of the candle . . .

COURTUMA:
No, Ona, it is not the heat of the candle but the fire of desire which your guest is fanning. Is an old bird caught with chaff?

DIAKU:
Jewel, I should be going now. Thank you and good night.

COURTUMA:
Thank God, you know you've overstayed your period of welcome.

DIAKU: *(to ONA as he takes up the Bible)*
Be on your guard. The hour of the Lord is close at hand. The Lord shall come like a thief in the middle of the night.

COURTUMA:

So long as he doesn't steal what belongs to me. You Christians and your Lord who forbids stealing and yet calls himself a thief. That's how he has taught you to steal people's daughters' virtues.

DIAKU:

No, sir, it doesn't mean that the Lord is a thief.

COURTUMA:

I don't need you, nymph that you are, to bore me with your Bible.

DIAKU: *(pretending not to notice the chief's displeasure)*

Well, Ona, as I was saying, the son of man may not come like a thief but may perch like a bird in your compound, chirping, "Ona, Ona" in the middle of the night. When that hour comes, do not run away, for then the hour of the Lord is close at hand. He knocks at your door, at your heart, and you must open to let him in. Prepare yourself for the Lord tomorrow. *(DIAKU rises to leave immediately)*

ONA: *(smiles knowingly)*

D'accord.

COURTUMA: *(angrily)*

Ona, what is wrong with you? The young man wants to go home. Why are you calling him back?

ONA:

Father, I did not call him back.

COURTUMA:

What? What I heard with my own ears just now? Son of Otu Agada, are you also teaching my daughter to tell white lies? Can you swear you didn't say "Diaku" just now?

ONA:

Father, *d'accord* in French means "agreed."

COURTUMA:

Hmm! *(ONA and DIAKU burst out laughing knowing that their strategy to confuse the old man has worked; their laughter angers the chief further. He is trying to tie his wrapper when it falls, pulling down the candle and the light. ONA and DIAKU seize the opportunity for a quick kiss as COURTUMA is about to rekindle the candle. He finds them glued together, lips together, and exclaims, biting his fingers)* Ona!

(The couple disengages) Diaku! Go before I open my eyes! Ona! Ona! Oh, Ona! Why? Why, why must you lick another man's spittle like the white man? *(Exit* DIAKU*)*

ONA:
Father, it is no spittle. It is an act of love.

COURTUMA:
Love? What symptom of love? No, Ona, I sent you to school not to contract the white man's disease but to learn his graces. When I served Mr. Whitely, he cursed me anytime I spat on my palm to rub on my chapped skin at harmattan. But Mr. Whitely always licked his wife's tongue and lips with all her cough. Whenever Mrs. Whitely coughed, you would think china was breaking. Tufia! Ona, how do you know that Agada's son has no disease in him that you are licking? May this be your last!
(Calming, he calls) Ona!

ONA:
Father!

COURTUMA:
Promise me you will never suck another man's tongue again.

ONA:
I will try not to. *(*COURTUMA *fetches a cup of water, hands it over to* ONA*)*

COURTUMA:
Then wash your mouth with this and go to bed. *(*ONA *obeys, lights fade out)*
(Blackout)

MOVEMENT FOUR

COURTUMA*'s house. A cock crows. Midnight. A knock at the door, and* ONA *stealthily walks up to open for* DIAKU.

ONA: *(speaking in low tone)*
Darling D. So you've come at last. I've been waiting restlessly. Every bird's voice I thought was your own. I kept wondering if you'd never come.

DIAKU:

My greatest fear was meeting your dad. Where is he?

ONA:

He's fast asleep . . . in his own bedroom.

DIAKU: *(falling on* ONA*'s bed)*

Fantastic! Great! Wonderful! For once I shall have my way, my way . . . Love! How I love and cherish you! *(He grabs* ONA *to himself, fondling)*

ONA:

But my father . . . my father.

DIAKU:

Your father? I'll take care of him. Put you in the family way, that's how to shut him up.

ONA:

That's because you're assuming that you could be faster than him.

DIAKU:

And do you doubt it? *(*ONA *is about to go and quench the candlelight when they hear a scream from* COURTUMA*'s room)*

COURTUMA:

Ona! Ona! Where are you going? What are you doing? *(At this point,* DIAKU *and* ONA *panic.* DIAKU *is turning into jelly. He jumps under the bed.* ONA *hangs down her bedspread to await her father any moment he enters.* COURTUMA *continues)* Ona! come. I am your father . . . I will confirm you—you with my own oil. Life-giving juice to anoint you. I, who gave you life. I can give you the cream and seed of life. Ona! Stop! Don't go. Don't do it, Do you doubt my power?

"Dominus vomitus."

Ona! Ona! my Jewel.

OLIAKU: *(startled voice)*

Isah-e-e! *Isah-e e!* My lord! my lord! What is wrong? Speak! Can't you speak?

COURTUMA: *(muffled voice)*

What?

OLIAKU:

You were screaming, saying many things.

COURTUMA:

Oh, I'm sorry, it's a nightmare.

OLIAKU:

And see how you're sweating. *(fairly long silence.* DIAKU *emerges from under the bed, claustrophobic, starts dressing up)*

ONA:

Oh, dear me! Can't take this any longer. Must this continue? Can't you come tomorrow to introduce our engagement to my parents?

DIAKU: *(fidgeting)*

Emm . . . Eem . . . I'll, I'll think about it . . . I'll think about it. See you soon.

(Exit DIAKU. ONA *pensive and groping and fiddling with the candlelight until light dims)*

MOVEMENT FIVE

Some days later. It is late afternoon. DIAKU *arrives at* COURTUMA's *house with his father,* OTU, *and their kinsmen. They come with a calabash of palm wine, a bottle of gin, and a head of tobacco sealed.*

In the parlor are DIAKU, OTU, *his kinsmen,* COURTUMA *and* OLIAKU. COURTUMA *sends for* ADAGOR *and* EKETE, *who come to join the group with surprised looks on their faces. As the conversation starts, the* JESTER *from* OTU's *village staggers in to join them uninvited.* OTU *and his people, embarrassed, try to send him out, but he refuses to go.*

OTU: *(clearing his throat)*

Ede, chief Courtuma Rapu, Rapu, son of Awali. They who scoop money like sand from the ground. They who can boast of knowing Oyibo more than the white man who owns it. I salute you. I salute you.

Ogwashi kwenu! *(three times and all respond.)* Kwenu! Kwenu!

Do I guess that everybody is well? Kwenu! Kwenu!

COURTUMA:

Of course, yes. Unless you don't wish us so.

OTU:

How can I, or do you mean to tell me that I am not welcome?

COURTUMA:

But I already welcomed you. *(coldly)* You are welcome.

OTU:

Well, my friend, Courtuma, I have always admired you— your courage, your fortitude, your honesty, and your grace. You have been a long-standing friend, and now my son here wishes to canonize that by what I hear. We have seen the beautiful flower in your compound, and we wish you let us pluck it.

*(*COURTUMA *ignoring them)*

COURTUMA: *(rubbing his palms and shaking his head)*

Hmm . . . Hmm . . . Hmm . . . *(scratches his head)*

OTU:

Ubulu Uku people say, "Ude yabulu okwu." Let the grunt take over speech.

COURTUMA:

Ona! Ona! *(turning to his wife)* Ehn, Oliaku, why don't you take Ona to see some of my relatives on Ogbenta today?

*(*ONA *rushing in from her room)*

ONA:

No, Father, I can't go today. Diaku and his father have come to see you about our . . .

COURTUMA:

Eh, your what . . . eh . . .

ONA:

Our engagement.

COURTUMA:

Enge—What?

ONA:

Engagement, Papa.

COURTUMA: *(tapping his foot on the floor)*

Enge-gi-menti. Enge-gi-ment. I, too, have my own engage-ment with you. Get inside and let's hear something else!

DIAKU:

But I've already given Jewel an engagement ring.

COURTUMA: *(laughing)*

Ooo, yaah-o. So that's what you call engagement? I see, I see. *(standing)* Now tell me, which schoolgirl doesn't wear an engagement ring nowadays? Engagement ring, wedding . . . What are they worth today? Both the free and the engaged wear them. They are now ten for one kobo. Just like women, too. With the magic of a ring, I can get as many as twenty women in a twinkle of an eye. Girls wear rings even without being given. Even your mother now wears one. I can't recall ever giving her any ring. *(turning to* OLIAKU) Did I also give you a ring?

OLIAKU:
Mba kwa-o!

COURTUMA:
No, Ona, my Jewel. You are too precious to be bought or bonded with a mere ring.

DIAKU:
But to Ona and myself that ring has a meaning.

COURTUMA:
To me, and me alone, it has no meaning.

OTU:
Courtuma, you surprise me. Whether these two children have or have not exchanged rings should not really matter to us. They have not yet bypassed our tradition. That is why I have come with my son and my kinsmen to start clearing the grounds for further negotiations on this marriage proposal. My kinsmen . . .

COURTUMA: *(pointing at the* JESTER *in disgust)*
Including this one? This imbecile, eh?

OTU:
Well, I did not come with him, but even then, was he not counted in the 1963 census?

COURTUMA:
Otu Agada, eh. Otu Agada, eh!

OTU:
Ehei.

COURTUMA: *(smiling sadly and shaking his head)*
Otu Agada, eh.

OTU:
Ehei.

COURTUMA:
I have heard what you said. We all have heard what you said. My kinsman here, Ekete, am I lie?

EKETE:
Mba . . . Mba—.

COURTUMA: *(still calmly and very subdued)*
Ehn, ehn, Otu Agada, you are not a child in Ogwashi Uku,
and even if someone comes to me in my sleep to ask me,
I will tell him that Otu Agada is a man in Aniocha and that
he knows the traditions. How can an elder be in the house
while a she-goat suffers the pain of labor under leash?

EKETE:
Otu Agada! What my brother is saying is right. It is we who
should teach the young ones about our tradition. That is
why my brother has to chew his words like an old man
chewing pepper fruit. Ona is an only child. *(COURTUMA,
nodding his head in agreement)*

OTU: *(nodding, too, and standing)*
Eziokwu. I understand what you mean. It is water which
drowns people. It is still water that people must drink. We
are not strangers in Aniocha. If the rhythm of a dance
changes, the steps change, too. You can see that our son
and daughter's skins have become lighter than ours because of the rays from the white man's land. We cannot
pretend that we don't know when darkness overtakes
light. I am a Christian, and I do not believe . . .
*(COURTUMA spitting in disgust, wipes the spittle with his
feet and stands up to leave. Exit COURTUMA, ONA trailing
him to return. She follows him into the bedroom. OLIAKU
follows shortly, leaving EKETE and the rest of the guests.
ONA soon reappears, looking dejected)*

ADAGOR: *(speaking to OTU and his kinsmen)*
No wonder they say you are a family of fools—osu. *(EKETE
tries to hush her, but she refuses to shut her mouth)*
Don't you know that Ona is an Idegbe and that she cannot
marry outside this family?

EKETE:
Adagor, shut up. These things are not said like that.

ONA *(angered)*
What? Me? Over my dead body. Never! Not while my eyes
can see the light of the day. Never!

EKETE: *(speaking to nobody in particular)*
You see now what you have done? I'm coming . . . *(Exit
EKETE, followed by ADAGOR, deserting the guests)*

OTU: *(resignedly)*
Well, my kinsmen, let us go home. The message is clear.
There is no harm in stealing cassava tubers. If one is

caught in the act, one simply returns home with one's ba-sin. *(Then, all rise including* JESTER, *who craves the palm wine in the calabash.* OTU's *wife attempts to carry the wine)*

OTU:

No, no, leave the wine. Our people's tradition must not be violated. Where the wine visits, there shall it stay. *(Exit. But soon the* JESTER *returns with his cup to partake of the rejected calabash of wine. Just then,* OLIAKU *is reen-tering. The* JESTER *notices her and runs off.* OLIAKU *lifting the calabash and calling* COURTUMA)

OLIAKU:

My lord.

COURTUMA: *(emerging)*

Hmm.

OLIAKU:

See, the strangers have gone and left the calabash. Let us carry it in and invite our kinsmen to drink.

COURTUMA: *(now angry)*

Do you take my kinsmen for vultures? *(*COURTUMA *hits* OLIA-KU's *hand. The calabash falls and breaks. Gong and drum in the background punctuated with sound of a dog barking. The sound invites* ONA *to the scene, includ-ing* EKETE, *all shocked and speechless.* UGO, *too, coinci-dentally is returning to the scene with* DIAKU *and two of the village dancers. The church bell rings, and simulta-neously the* TOWN CRIER *is heard making the following announcement)*

TOWN CRIER:

Kom! Kom! Kom!

Ogawashi eboiteeni. A strange thing has happened in our land.

At Abuano, as the market was in its fullness today, a cock crowed

in the market. Who owns this cock? In whose domain does

this animal dwell? Our Omu is enraged. Prepare. Prepare.

Prepare to purge our gods scandalized. Seven market days from

now, the next moon will be out. Then will the earth drink. This

is the message. A message does not kill its bearer—o. *Kom!*

(Exit TOWN CRIER *followed by a group of ritual dancers who dance round the broken calabash.* ONA, COURTUMA, *and* OLIAKU *in a circle. The dance is very brief. Exit dancers, each throwing a palm frond on the broken pieces of the calabash.* OLIAKU, *now incensed, takes up her broomstick)*

OLIAKU:
Isah! Leave Ona alone! Leave my one yam seed alone. Let me plant and eat the new yam like the rest of the world. Egbebelu Ugo belu-Isah. Let me bear the burden alone . . . leave Ona alone . . .

(As OLIAKU *goes off,* COURTUMA, *looking morose, stands in front of his shrine.* EKETE *comes into the yard unannounced.* COURTUMA *startled)*

COURTUMA: *(sighing, recovers himself)*
So it is you, Ekete? How are my children?

EKETE: *(not raising his face from the ground)*
They are well.

COURTUMA:
I wonder, or is your wife at it again?

EKETE:
Nobody is "at" anything but you, Courtuma.

COURTUMA: *(interrupting)*
Hmm.

EKETE:
Courtuma!

COURTUMA:
Hmm.

EKETE:
Did I hear you broke the calabash of wine brought by Otu Agada and his son to marry Ona?

COURTUMA:
Yes, but what is wrong about that?

EKETE:
Courtuma, Courtuma.
Remember, remember the tse-tse fly perched on the scrotum . . . Courtuma. Ona is an Idegbe, we know. But that does not mean we must beg the ground to let us stand on it. You broke the calabash of wine. Now, how do you think you can save one tradition by breaking another? Did you not send Ona to school? The tse-tse fly on the scrotum . . .

(Before he completes this, cock crows and the DIBIA *walks in threateningly. Exit* EKETE*)*

DIBIA: *(chanting as he sprays nzu on the right and sand on the left)*
Emene, Emene
Adia egbu ogoli
A set tradition does not kill a bride
A barrage of stones does not kill the pear tree
The vulture is not beaten by rain in its nest
The squirrel's child is never born dumb
Ine is for each year. Each youth is for Ine.
As we did last year
So shall we this year . . .
Every year, every year
The day and then the night
The day and then the night . . .
(As he says the final part, he notices COURTUMA *eaves-dropping; the plate of nzu falls from him. Angered, he raises his hand to strike* ONA, *then changes his mind. He shrugs his shoulder, biting his lip, warning)*
Courtuma! Courtuma, be advised and save your face.

Do not scratch the itching eye with what you scratch the ear. *(With each word, the* DIBIA *moves nearer* COURTUMA, *who in turn retreats until he flees from the* DIBIA *in fear)*
(Blackout)

MOVEMENT SIX

COURTUMA's *sitting room.* ONA *and* COURTUMA *and* OLIAKU *are seated.*

COURTUMA:
Hmm, eh . . . eh.

Yes, my Jewel. I have called you to talk to you about some important issues. First, I must apologize to you for what you may call my cruelty to Diaku and his father, Otu, and

yourself. I was compelled by circumstances to do
so . . . I had to.

ONA:

You didn't have to.

COURTUMA:

Ona!

ONA:

Yes?

COURTUMA:

Do you realize you are an only child?

ONA:

Yes, I do, and why must I be reminded of that every time?

COURTUMA:

You have to, because that means that we are nothing without you. It means that my fathers thought it wise not to
allow our homestead to be deserted after I'm gone. And
you, Ona, are the living plant to shade this homestead.
How are you going to shade it, Ona? Answer me.

ONA:

I do not know.

COURTUMA:

Then I must let you know, because you are still a child.
Our people say that what kills the old is to know without
letting the youth know, and what kills youth is to hear
without heeding advice from the old. He who has an only
child owes the Earth a debt.

ONA:

Father, I do not understand you.

COURTUMA:

OK, then. What this simply means is that you, my Ona,
cannot marry outside this my family. You are an Idegbe!

ONA: *(flabbergasted)*

What!

COURTUMA:

Yes, you can neither marry nor bear children for any
other man.

ONA:

Impossible! Father, for once let me say no to you.
Capital NO!

COURTUMA:

Ona, take it easy now. Take it . . .

ONA:

No, Father. Not easy now. I have always succumbed to you, that is why you have messed me up. My whole life has been messed up by you because I love you. All my life has been circumscribed by you just because you own me. Now all those knots you have tied into my life to ensure my perpetual bondage to you must be untied.

COURTUMA:

Ona! Ona!!

ONA:

Leave me alone. Do I not see my mates? Am I to live my life unfulfilled just because I am your only child and you have some obsolete tradition?

COURTUMA:

Ona, hear me.

ONA:

I refuse to hear.

OLIAKU:

You refuse to hear your father? Obida forbids! Isah! Come! They have cast a spell on my only child, Ona?

ONA:

A spell? Nobody has cast any spell on me. If anything, it is your own spell. For once, I must let you understand this—the fact that you gave me life does not mean you must control it. Did you not choose each other for marriage?

OLIAKU: *(bursting into bitter laughter and clapping her hands)*

Ona, you really amuse me. My parents gave me to your father as wife. I didn't have to choose him. But you have a choice. I didn't even know him. He used to come to my father at times to help him in the farm. I thought they were friends. Then, one day, I was told that they had come to pay my dowry. But Ona, yours is different. You have a choice.

ONA:

Between my father and who?

OLIAKU:

No, not between your father and anybody. But a choice to bear children for your father alone or marry a wife who can help bear children to multiply the stock.

ONA:

I see. You people have a very ambitious murder plan. You will not only slaughter me on the altar of your decadent tradition, but would also want another female head. I say to hell with your tradition. Homestead! Norm! All!

Let the wind blow—let the shaky homestead be blown. Anything that cannot stand the force of change must be uprooted or be blown into oblivion by the storm heralding the new season!

COURTUMA:

No, Ona . . . you don't understand.

ONA:

And is that why you must tear me apart? If your sole aim is to make me remain at home and breed children for you, why did you chase Diaku away? Or must I not also love whoever must give me those children?

COURTUMA:

Diaku belongs to a family of Osu. Our blood must not be polluted.

ONA:

As if it will never be polluted. If I'm kept at home to bear children for my father or marry a wife, either way, it won't be pure blood. Which child is born from pure blood of his family anyway? Even if you had a son and he had an exogamous marriage, the blood will even be less pure. Tell me, Father and Mother, if you graft an orange seedling into a grapefruit seedling, is the offspring still the same pure orange or grapefruit?

COURTUMA:

Hmm . . . No. No.

ONA:

So, you see, to prevent me from marrying or forcing me to marry a wife cannot solve the problem.

COURTUMA:

It can, because your children or your wife must answer your father's name. If you are kept at home, any man coming to you knows so already and can never claim paternity of those children.

ONA:

Then the system indirectly encourages prostitution.

COURTUMA:

It is far from prostitution. The society sanctions it.

ONA:

So the other is prostitution simply because society does not sanction it, and even though it is the same process that is involved?

COURTUMA:

I assure you that within the system, it will still be my blood. Are you not my daughter? And does my blood not flow in you? Likewise, any child you bear for me has already been branded and infused with my blood. The homestead . . . Ona. The root . . . Ona . . .

ONA:

All must come down! If the homestead is too shaky, it must come down with the storm. If the tree's root is not firm, let it show its face to the sky. *(Voice of* TOWN CRIER *can be heard from afar)*

TOWN CRIER: *(frightening)*

Courtuma, Courtuma, the moon will soon be out. It shall be full, but it shall be red. A new season comes, Courtuma. Let the wind blow, Courtuma. Can you see the moon planted in the sky, Courtuma? Can you see it seated with the tip of its head? Courtuma? Who poured oil on the moon? Can't you leave Ona alone? Courtuma, Courtuma, can't you speak? *(*COURTUMA *almost shivering and shrinking from fright until voice stops and lights fade out)*

MOVEMENT SEVEN

Sundown. COURTUMA'S *sitting room.* ONA *sits feebly on a chair.* OLIAKU *walks in, gives her a letter.* ONA *glances at the address, her face lights up. She opens letter.*

ONA: *(stroking her chest, saying with excitement)*

Oh, Diaku, Diaku, ever loving darling . . . *(then freezes and reads)* Ugo? Diaku? Married? Diaku, Ugo married? *(She breaks down sobbing. The more she mutters the two names, the more hysterical she becomes. But slowly, the truth dawns on her, and she makes her resolution)* Yes, yes, my father has at last succeeded in ruining my life. But I will show him. Ona will show him pepper . . . Yes, yes, I am going to implicate him . . . Yes . . . Yes . . . The wheel must come right round . . . *(Light slowly fades into the next scene with* ONA *seen lying unconscious on the floor. Outside the house, the* JESTER, *completely soaked in palm wine, talks to himself. He carries a keg of palm wine)*

JESTER:

Manya, you are so fine, you are so fine. I like the way you shack. Manya, you are so fine. I like the way you shack *(staggers, drops the keg of palm wine)* It is four moons since Ona, the Jewel of Courtuma, went back to school. Yesterday, she was rushed back home from school. They say she is sick. She has been sick for some time. What can a young girl be sick of? Rheumatism? Arthritis . . . of the womb? Or is she suffering from the hangover of abortion which our girls have perfected nowadays? But Ona has been a good girl. I have never seen her paint her lips like those of the girls who walk on their toes and talk "Psi—psi" like people with yaws on their lips. And have you seen Ona's body? Have you seen how her waist and chest have grown, or has Ona the beautiful one joined these birds that whitewash their skin? I fear. I fear for Ona. The full moon is emerging. The season's end approaches. Will Ona join us at the festival to satirize those who have defiled the land? Will the land be purged? And the new season see its new yam? Anyway, which one concerns me? Palm wine go still flow. But what noise do I hear from Courtuma's big house: "Dibia . . . Dibia . . ."
Hmm. See Dibia going to Courtuma's house. "We go see today."

OLIAKU:

Courtuma! Water! Water *(COURTUMA brings water. He, too, is trembling like a reed in the storm. He pours the water on ONA)*

COURTUMA:

Obida forbids. Ngene forbids.

OLIAKU:

Help! Help, my only child, my only hope.

COURTUMA:

Ona! Ona! Water! Egg! Oliaku! Oliaku! Bring water! Bring egg! Rain doesn't beat the vulture in its nest.

OLIAKU:

The priest! The high priest, the oracle!

COURTUMA:

Go immediately and consult the oracle.

(Exit OLIAKU. *Returns shortly with the* DIBIA. *The* DIBIA *unpacks his tools and spreads them on the ground, asks for water for absolution. The* DIBIA *is dressed in red, and his eyes are powdered across with white chalk called nzu.* COURTUMA's *house still.* ONA *is seen lying lifelessly on the floor. The* DIBIA's *oracular pronouncements)*

DIBIA:

Obala Otule.
I say go here
It doesn't go.
Go there it doesn't go.
The road is forked.
I stand on crossroads.

Courtuma, it was your cock that crowed at the market-place at noon? *(*COURTUMA *aghast) Can* you stop water flowing downward from the head? *Can* a man stop the cause of destiny? The tree must fall. All you can do to help in its life is simply to prop it up. But fall the tree must, because the wind is too strong. Now the sacred tree is falling, what can man do? A sheep with only a ram as its child is childless, so the gods pronounced.

COURTUMA:

I do not understand.

DIBIA:

Then let Ona speak for herself. *(He sprinkles some liquid on* ONA. ONA *rises immediately, alert)* Here she comes. Let Ona talk for herself. Ona, tell us what ails you. *(silence)* Ona, be bold. Tell your father what ails you.

*(*ONA *indicating that she is pregnant by pointing at her womb)*

ALL:

What? Who is responsible? Who is the man? *(silence)*

DIBIA:

Tell us, Ona, your life is in danger. *(silence)*

OLIAKU:

Speak, speak, my Jewel, we will not be angry with you, whoever is responsible. You know that's the heart's desire of your father, to have a grandchild by his Ona.

COURTUMA: *(relieved, goes inside, brings another bead and puts it on his neck. He begins to snuff. Then later continues the question)*

Ona, do you fear I might be angry with you? No, Ona, tell me, for the boundless joy is mine. I, Eloke, Courtuma, a grandfather to my Ona's children . . .

ONA:

You, my father, are the cause.

COURTUMA: *(wide-eyed)*

I?

ONA: *(boldly)*

Yes, you are the cause.

OLIAKU: *(running berserk into the street)*

Obida Obu Ogwe! Isha come, come. Come and hear. *(As this is going on, the DIBIA is busy packing his tools into his bag to make sure he runs away before people rush in)*

COURTUMA:

Ona, Ona, please, whatever you want. Whatever you ask. I must do it for you. But for God's sake, name another man. Ona, please. My life is in your hands. Ona, please save my ebbing life. Say it is Diaku. Let me fetch you Diaku. Diaku will marry you. Let Diaku marry you. Now, now . . .

ONA: *(snappishly)*

Diaku has married Ugo.

COURTUMA:

Then, Ona, name another man. Ona, why must you strangle me, I who loved you so?

ONA:

Your love has landed me where I am.

COURTUMA:

Ona, it is not me, but who will believe me? Ona, I am your father. Remember the homestead. Ona, Ona.

ONA:

That I remember, and that is why you're the father of my child. You asked for it, and you got it.

COURTUMA:

Ona! Ona! Oh, my love has choked me. The stick I chew in my mouth has chewed me. Ona, Ona, Ona *(COURTUMA walks backward into the room and begins to exit into a bush path in the village. He pulls off his beads, drops them on the floor at ONA'S feet, looking very pensive. Then, biting his lips and fingers, goes off, head bowed down. ONA picks up the beads. A woman returning from the market carrying her wares runs across in a state of frenzy and drops her wares. ONA still looking lost. OLIAKU running to ONA, startled)*

OLIAKU:

Ona, where is your father?

(no reply) Where has your father gone, leaving his beads here?

(ONA points toward the street COURTUMA disappeared into. Then the TOWN CRIER behind announces the epilogue. As the announcement is made, OLIAKU runs into the direction where ONA has pointed. ONA, now realizing what has happened, picks up COURTUMA'S beads in fear. She clutches them feverishly. With each sentence from the TOWN CRIER, she runs toward the crucifix and then toward the shrine. She continues running between the two as if torn between them until lights fade out on her)

EPILOGUE

TOWN CRIER: *(with a gong)*
Kom! Kom! Kom!

Isah!

The moon is full
The old season dies. A new crop is sown. What harvest do you foresee? Today is the climax of the festival ending the drudgery of the old season. The new yam will be eaten, but it is streaked with blood. At sundown, Courtuma, son of Awali-ego, took his own life.

May the gods forbid it. Yes, the great Courtuma, son of Awali-ego, those who measure money with baskets have

fouled our air, and his body must not touch the good
Earth like his peers. Take his body to the bad bush and
pour no libation on it for his soul to ever wander the sur-
face of the Earth and not rest with his fathers. And shall
we eat the new yam with blood? Why must they turn our
rite to tears? Must we allow them to pour ashes and sand
on the grounds we sweep at Ine?

(As TOWN CRIER *announces,* VILLAGE WOMEN *assemble in
mournful state, dancing and circling round* COURTUMA's
*house ritualistically. This is punctuated with drum and
dirge, which continue for a while, with* ONA *confused,
quivering, and running between the shrine and the crucifix. Light dims, lingers on, and focuses on* ONA—*alone.
The light never goes out completely*)

Parables
for a
Season

A Word from the Author

AMONG OTHER INTERPRETATIONS,

"PARABLES FOR A SEASON" IS

AN EXTENDED METAPHOR ON

THE SIGNIFICANT PLACE AND ROLE OF

WOMEN AS UNIVERSAL PILLARS FOR

STABILITY IN TIMES OF SOCIO-

POLITICAL STRESS AND TRANSITION.

CAST

OGISO: *The king who is preparing to abdicate the throne because he does not have a son to succeed him*

TAIDE: *Princess*

INE: *Princess*

TUFA: *Princess*

SOTIMO: *Commoner*

ADAMAWA: *Commoner*

OZOMA: *Chief, a foreigner whose hard work and high achievement have earned him a chieftancy title*

IYASE: *Chief*

IDEHEN: *Chief*

ANEHE: *Queen*

WA: *Queen*

BIA: *Queen*

ZO: *One of the queens who later becomes the regent of Idu, and she is called Wazobia*

OLD TERMITE: *zo's mother*

CHORUS OF IDU: *Includes* TOWN CRIER, *children, drummers, commoners (In order to reduce the cast, some of the major characters can play double roles)*

FIRST COMMONER

SECOND COMMONER

THIRD COMMONER

PROLOGUE

Stage opens onto the kingdom of Idu. At the center is the village square. From afar one can see silhouettes of huts flanking sides of the village square. But right behind the center of the square, an imposing mansion sits. Spotlight reveals that even though the sides of the building are designed in mud color, some part of the roofing is made of metals, rods, corrugated iron sheets, while yet another part is made up of thatch. But conspicuously evident is the righthand side of the building which is yet to be completed. Around the building are scraps of metal, artifacts, thatch, raffia, nails, iron sheets, etc., suggesting that the house is in a transitional stage of construction. Slow rhythm of drumming combined with mournful tunes of the flute or horn intermittently penetrating the otherwise quiet background. The tension is so thick, one can cut it. The air seems thick, foreboding, and pregnant. Suddenly tearing the apparent calm is the shrill sound of the gong followed by the coarse voice of the TOWN CRIER, *subduing all other sounds in the background.*

TOWN CRIER:
Termites of Idu!
Termites of Idu!
Termites of Idu!
Sit with your ears,

Walk with your heads and hands,
Till the earth with your eyes and legs.
Termites of Idu,
Is the gong ever dumb?
Termites of Idu,
Can a single grain fill a basket?
Termites of Idu,
Can a single tree make a forest?
Termites of Idu,
The sun which rises in the morning
Must set in the evening,
The sun which rises from the East
Must set in the West.
Termites of Idu,
Come . . . come . . . come
Join as one
To build . . . to plant . . . to reap.
Termites of Idu,
Come . . . come . . . come,
Each one with hoe,
Each one with cutlass . . .
(The rhythm of the horn increases in tempo. More lights.)

MOVEMENT ONE

(At this point, the termites of Idu begin to assemble in trickles; some with hoes, some with ladders, etc. They begin to climb to the top of the uncompleted building, while some, especially children, assist in gathering the debris on the ground as others convey building materials to those building on the rooftop. Work beings in earnest. As the assembly increases in strength, the rhythm of the horn decreases, and soon the voice of the TOWN CRIER *gains ascendancy)*

TOWN CRIER:
Termites of Idu,
The seed yam planted

And left in the earth rots.
Termites of Idu,
The seed yam planted
And left in the soil
Turns harvest for beetles.
Termites! Termites! Termites of Idu!
There's a time to sow,
A time to reap . . .
(From this point, the chorus of termites, particularly their children, assembles and takes up the refrain)

TOWN CRIER:
A time to till.

CHORUS:
A time to weed.

TOWN CRIER:
A time to tear.

CHORUS:
A time to mend.

CHORUS:
A time to come.

TOWN CRIER:
A time to go.

CHORUS:
A time to begin.

TOWN CRIER:
A time to end.

CHORUS:
A time to wake.

TOWN CRIER:
A time to sleep.

CHORUS:
A time to laugh.

TOWN CRIER:
A time to weep.

CHORUS:
A time, a time, a time, a time . . .
*(*CHORUS *subsides)*

TOWN CRIER:
Termites of Idu,
Shadows are getting long.
Time, time to gather.
I can see silhouettes of men,

I see shadows
Gather to give shape to shadows,
Gather to gather yesterday's debris.
So says the king . . .

CHORUS:

A time, a time, a time.
(The refrain is repeated by the CHORUS *of termites and their children. Next, the children begin another song about the two legendary women who vied for owner-ship of one child during the reign of King Solomon)*

OGISO:

It is no time for long greeting
When the sun sets fast on us.
It is no time to tarry
When shadows take the shape of palm trees.
It is no time to smile
When the sun meets the Earth
And men's bowels threaten to empty
All hope.
It is no time to tarry.
Idu,
A time comes when the pear fruit
Ripens and must fall.
A time comes when the coconut laden
With milk goes on its downward journey
In ascent of powers above.
Idu,
Now is the twilight of hope.
The rain comes, gives way to harmattan,
The rain comes, makes way for harmattan,
The sun shines, makes way for rain.
In the cycle of comings and goings,
In the cycle of comings and goings,
Now is our season of exit.
What begins ends,
What ends begins.
Tomorrow, we make our exit.

CHORUS:

What?
Are you leaving us?
Stay, king,
Our great king,
Stay.

ADAMAWA:

You started so well. Tarry awhile.
Let the fruits you have so
Devotedly tended ripen,
My king . . .

OGISO:

Our dear ones
Learn the logic of living
In our commune.
Many times, some plant
That others may harvest,
And in the relay of existence
The one that begins
Is usually not the one that ends,
And the one that ends
Is usually not the one that begins.
That's part of life's checks and balances.
It's the cycle.
Check this column of ants . . .
(He points to a column of ants in a relay; some re-turning, carrying back food, others just on their way, empty but businesslike)

OGISO:

Tomorrow
We begin our longer journey,
Our ascension to higher orbits.
Pray the wind is light to bear us swift
And aloft
In exploration of other lands
Our journey of hope

CHORUS:

Ewo-o-o-o-o.

TAIDE:

But why?

INE:

Why?

TUFA:

Why?

CHORUS:

Why? Why? Why? *(Echo of "Why" fills the air)*

OGISO:

Ine!

INE: *(coming forward)*
Yes, Father!
OGISO:
Can your tender bosom
Withstand the scourge of
This hot seat of the throne
INE:
Hmm . . .
OGISO:
You will have time enough to chew that.
Tufa!
TUFA:
Father!
OGISO:
And your gentle voice
Calm the bloody thirst of this wild
Generation?
TUFA:
Perhaps, if given the time . . .
OGISO:
Aha! there you go . . .
Time! Time! Time . . .
Taide! You too?
TAIDE:
Time is the great trainer.
OGISO:
Yes, with time, the young palm
Grows into a tree.
(OGISO looks at the pregnant queen, BIA)
ADAMAWA:
King, perhaps you
May wait a while.
Behind those heavy clouds
May come rain.
OGISO:
I have seen
Seasons and seasons of clouds
Come and go,
But there's always
Been a shower,
Just a shower,
But no real rain comes.

Perhaps my exit
May seed the sky
For rain enough
That tubers may sprout.

OZOMA:

King, you leave us naked.
Clothe us with your warmth,
Let your presence
Shield us from stray
Stones thrown here and
There by the mob of aspirants.

OGISO:

One does not watch a
Thrilling dance from
One spot alone.
And of course a tree
Which must grow must make
Room for branches.
A tree which must grow
Must shed brown leaves
In time and tune for
Green leaves
—*So be it!*
Tomorrow, the king
Makes his exit.

ZO:

What happens to us
When you're gone,
My lord?

CHORUS:

Yes, what happens to us?

OGISO:

That is the greater question!

IYASE:

That question does not arise.

ADAMAWA:

What do you mean,
That question does not arise?

IYASE:

Termites have always built
Palaces of mud.

There are always termites,
Come rain, come sun.
Kings, like rain, come in seasons.

IDEHEN:
And seasons come and go.

OGISO:
Kings reign all the same.

IYASE:
King's reign—
Only for a season,
Only for a season.

OZOMA:
Palaces remain for all seasons.

IYASE:
Not when they are fashioned
With mud, brittle, caky . . .

OGISO:
That will do,
Iyase!
You taunt me further . . . and . . .
And . . .

IYASE:
That is small matter.
When fire is gone,
Ashes are packed away.

OGISO:
That will do now.
Zo only asked a question.

IYASE:
And we only gave an answer.

ZO:
My lord, please stay awhile.

IYASE: *(fiercely)*
How dare you speak,
Woman that you are, in a
Gathering of men?

ZO: *(sarcastically)*
Woman and yet in a man's shoes.
The broomstick is nothing,
But each morning

The ones that matter
Seek it to clean their dirt.

OZOMA:
Of course, it does!

OGISO:
Termites of Idu!
When mother goes to market,
The breast milk travels with her,
But she leaves food enough
For the feeding of the baby at home.
The question is,
Will the ward left to feed the child
Burn it in the hearth?
Devour it? Or leave the child to starve?
(calling) Anehe!

ANEHE: *(rising)*
Yes, my lord!

OGISO:
That is a riddle for you.
Toughen your hands
That what we have started
Together remains.

ANEHE:
Your grace, my lord.
I will forever preserve your interest.

OGISO:
Wa!

WA:
My lord!

OGISO:
You, too.
I charge you to do all
For the glory of posterity.
Zo!

ZO: *(very emotional)*
Lord!

OGISO:
Gird your loins.
Bia!
(BIA, *in a near hysterical state, throws herself forward
and crumbles down on her knees)*

BIA: *(tearfully)*
My lord,
My lord,
Are you leaving me, too?
Do you leave me
For wolves to feed on?
Take me . . . take me . . .
Take me . . . Please . . .

OGISO:
My lovely one,
There are many acts
A man must perform alone.
Some he can share
And some he cannot share,
Like coming . . . like going,
Like birth.
Tell me, Bia,
What is the sex of that child you are carrying?

BIA:
I cannot . . .

OGISO: *(interrupting)*
Ohoo!
When is your hour of
Delivery?
Can you tell?
But come, it must
When it must come,
At the appointed hour,
You alone must deliver it
Safe and alive, alone . . .

BIA: *(interrupting)*
Don't say . . .
My king . . .
(She breaks down sobbing and then makes her exit)

OZOMA:
King,
Your parables
Are for a generation
With imagination on wings.
Ours is a generation
With thick scum on our ears.

King, speak! Speak! Speak
To us . . .

OGISO: *(smiling, calmly)*
Men are born alone
And paced out,
And the height of office
Prolongs distances.
Men are born alone.
On lonely paths they tread,
And alone they part.

OZOMA:
King,
Your voice sounds
Distant.

ADAMAWA:
Speak to us as one to the deaf.

OGISO:
Hah, my faithful ones,
certainly ours seems like a
Conversation
Between the deaf and the dumb.
Now, my faithful ones
(pointing to the uncompleted monument),
That is our mound,
A nest we have together labored for.
Now I depart. Will you allow storm
Into the nest?
Will you together join hands?
From violent winds protect it?
(As KING *rises, he takes off his very large shoes and crown and begins to show the gathering the uncompleted part of the building. He takes about three steps, stops, his hand in midair as he shows them the work ahead. Solemnly)*

OGISO:
This is tree planted,
I can see fruits coming,
But they are green,
Oh, so green!
Will you let it mature to seed?
Will you nurture it to seed?

And from the seed more fruits
May come for others yet to come?
Will you?
There
Fast winds blow and toss the seat.
Storm . . . storm . . . storm.
Oh, you generation of the deaf
Who have eyes to see
But cannot see beyond your nose.
Storm . . . storm . . . storm!
Engineered by you! You!
Oh, you generation of the deaf,
You *alone* can subdue storm.
My black generation,
Subdue storm to wind,
You alone can protect
That seat from storm
And the scourge of the sun.
You! You! You! Trap,
Trap your own destiny
In your fist.
Oh, you termites,
My black generation,
Small, small as you are,
Grow now! Grow!
Hear with your eyes,
See with your ears,
Walk tall with your heads,
Walk tall with your hands.
Idu . . . Idu . . . Idu.
(He takes about three steps, stops. Takes another step.
Brief silence. Then drum begins in slow rhythm. He
takes three steps backward. He looks faraway and nos-
talgic. He begins to depart backward)

OZOMA:
Farewell, great architect.

ADAMAWA:
Farewell, great builder.

OZOMA:
Farewell, farewell . . .
This monument, your
Emblem,

Your name engraved in gold
From head to tail of our kingdom,
Will forever glitter in the eyes
Of generations and generations
And generations yet to come.

ADAMAWA:
Your words of wisdom
Shall pierce the encrustation
Of deaf walls of these ears,
Echoing as sirens through
The strings of time.
(He takes up the large shoes) These large shoes left here
will need
A colossus with crutches to wear them
Well . . .
For now, farewell . . . farewell . . .

CHORUS:
Farewell!
Farewell!
*(King steadily now begins to recede backward. He looks
nostalgically at the uncompleted building. As he departs, the children sing sad tunes. Following after him
as if seeing him off are* IYASE, IDEHEN, OZOMA, ADAMAWA, WA,
COMMONERS, *etc. Drum and xylophone increase in tempo,
rise to a crescendo, and come to an abrupt stop. Everyone is gone. Only the queens remain. Silence.* ANEHE,
*breaking the silence, goes to spy on all corners of the
square to ensure that no one is eavesdropping on them.
Her manner of strutting betrays her happiness at the*
KING's *departure. Suddenly, she begins to scold the
other queens)*

ANEHE:
For God's sake, why this
Thick air around us—eh?
Is someone dead?
(No reply)
I say, answer me,
Or has Ogun, the god of iron, smelted
Your lips together forever?
*(No reply. She eyes them and suddenly goes into fits of
laughter, stops abruptly)*
Look at them! Look at them!

You who live in thin air
Think that forever you'll stay wrapped
Up in the cocoon of power.
Ha! Ha! Ha! Ha!
Listen, my queeeeeeeeeens . . .
Queens, queens indeed.
Males are like bees.
They suck from nectar to nectar.

ZO:
Females are no better, either,
Opening up their petals
For every probing bee to sap . . .

ANEHE: *(turning to* BIA*)*
You think we are now
Equal because the king raised
You to his shoulder against
The will of everyone else?
Look, my Queen B,
Count the silver strands on my
Head and you'll certainly know that
She who cooks longer can boast
Of more broken pots.
Yours is just beginning—I have
More broken as I've passed
Through the fingers of many kings.
Listen, my fairy queens.
Loving a king, a man of power,
Is like loving palm wine brewed fresh
And sweet. It soon intoxicates, or,
More likely, goes sour and stale,
But more—just as the drinker
Savors the pleasure of a good wine, so
He savors you and me.
The one who holds power is a
connoisseur—he sniffs it from air
To air and elopes in the direction
Where it is sweetest.
Ha ha ha ha.
Oh, generation of the deaf!
How much longer must I tell
You that power is nothing but high tide?
It soon rises, but it ebbs, too.

How much longer? Where is that fat
Cow, Bia—ugh—she certainly thought
The king would take her along. Ugh—kingly
Favors! That's how he fattens us all,
And once he's flattened of desire abandons
Us to labor alone . . .

BIA:

Please, leave me alone!
Stop taunting me with your
Rancid envy.
I know you'll slaughter ten cows
Now to celebrate the king's abdication.

ANEHE:

Oh certainly, certainly,
My Queen B,
You think mine is heart without nerves . . .

ZO:

Just because you were not his favorite.

ANEHE:

And you thought I smiled each
Night he flew from my bed like a
Fly to perch on yours
Even when they were my own days?
(At this point, WA *arrives)*

WA: *(interrupting)*

Men of power certainly have their
Favorites,
And like they explore women
They finger through
Counting the smears until
A power beyond them forces them
To downpour . . .
Kings come and go—
Will always come and go—
But the kingdom remains.

ZO: *(now rising up in anger)*

Yes, we know the kingdom remains,
But for whom?
To whom? Your kind?
You who won't even wait for a
Batting of the eye for your husband
To step out before you begin . . .

ANEHE:

I say swallow that trash before Idigwu
Spears you down! Swallow it . . .
(She approaches menacingly, and WA *comes between
them to arbitrate. Brief silence)*
Thank God after all that upon all your
Sleepless nights and endless pounding
You, too, were not able to give the
King a son—
Shame on you, snatcher!

WA:

Yes, now you prick the sensitive spot,
My dear coquettes . . .
Power is a traveler . . .
It goes where it pleases.
The truth is that we all failed,
We all failed.

ZO:

No, I didn't fail!

ANEHE:

If you didn't, why couldn't you
Give the king a son?

ZO:

The system,
It's the system.

ANEHE:

Ho ho ho.
The system! The system made her
Half-productive!

WA:

Oh, you generation of the deaf!
Stop haggling!
The king has left you a task—unite,
Join hands for its completion instead
Of pecking one another like silly hens.
Unite and plan solidly for the
Construction ahead.
(At this point, IYASE, *unnoticed by the queens, arrives on
the scene)*

IYASE: *(interrupting)*

And you think it's the likes
Of you who can complete the task?

(They all kneel in reverence to him)
Get you gone! You less than females!
For years we have labored to serve
And fatten you.
Now is the end of your rope as I begin
To climb mine.
(He changes mood suddenly, feigns friendliness)
Oh, I'm sorry for these
Harsh words. I shall indeed thank you for
facilitating my task—
To make my ascension so easy.
(He begins to strut as king; he goes to the throne, hovers around it, stops, looks at the construction work ahead, and bursts out laughing)

IYASE:
Work . . .
Construction.
We are sons of the soil.
(pointing at the throne)
Here is where we belong,
And they who are here by our grace,
The construction is their rent for
Tenancy.
We shall sit right here while
The sweat from their brow shall be
The juice for our anointment.
Ha ha ha ha . . .
(He touches the queens seductively. ANEHE *and* WA *rise and respond immediately, but* ZO *departs in anger. He ropes his hands around their necks. He is sandwiched between them and continues laughing until lights fade)*

MOVEMENT TWO

TOWN CRIER:
Termites of Idu,
Masters,

Masters who sift the womb of the
Earth and yet mold monuments of
It,
Builders and destroyers all at once,
Join hands for the construction before
Us.
Termites of Idu,
This season, our journey begins.
Rats inherit thrones built and
Deserted by men
That darkness may not envelop our
Kingdom. Termites of Idu,
Hold your lanterns in view
That the sound of darkness may not be
Pulled across your eyes,
Gird your loins that darkness
May not envelop our kingdom.
Kings come and go.
Unite! Unite! That our monument may
Outlast us.
Seven market days from now,
The transition begins.
A king-surrogate to sit on our
Empty throne must be found,
Until three seasons when the
Worthy one to wear the crown
Must be enthroned,
So says the oracle.
This is the message,
I am only the bearer—o!
*(The assembly of males begins to gather again. Every
individual brings his implements. They exchange pleas-
antries and soon begin work. The most prominent
among them are* OZOMA, ADAMAWA, *and* SOTIMO. *Others as-
sist them, sending them metals, sand, etc., from the
ground)*

OZOMA:
You're up already?

ADAMAWA:
Oh yes! This is not time for
Snorting in sleep.

SOTIMO: *(arriving)*
Indeed the time calls for one to
Be on wings.

OZOMA:
Lest we crawl and get "hen-pecked."

ADAMAWA:
And with the pronouncement.

SOTIMO:
Which pronouncement? You self!
You smell fart even before it
Is released from the stomach!

OZOMA:
My friend, you stop pretending. Were
You not with me when the town crier
sounded . . .

SOTIMO: *(interrupting)*
Oh that?
Of course, I heard it,
But how does it concern me?

ADAMAWA: *(jokingly)*
My dear, I don't blame you.
After all, we're not kingmakers.

OZOMA: *(laughing)*
Like some of us here can boast of.
Oh, I know these so-called king-
Makers have been having sleepless
Nights, scheming, planning intrigues,
Devastating barriers others have worked
So hard to build, just to discredit
Them and install themselves king.

ADAMAWA:
By the grace of past favors.

OZOMA:
What do you mean by past favors?
Numerical strength?

SOTIMO:
Precisely, Ozoma.
That's the tragedy of our times,
That issues are not considered on
Merit but on solidarity, numerical

Strength and atavistic concepts
Of race and superiority.

ADAMAWA:

It makes nonsense of democracy.

SOTIMO and OZOMA:

Democracy? Ho ho ho!

OZOMA:

Who talks of democracy in this land
Where even the strongest is threatened
With cancerous worms?

SOTIMO:

Ours is a kangaroo democracy . . . we are democrazy . . .
If there's anything like that . . .

ADAMAWA:

In any case, they need a king-
Surrogate. That means there'll
Be an election. Fair enough.

SOTIMO:

Foul!

OZOMA:

Their winners are appointed before
The elections are conducted. And
Like a herd of cattle, they zero in
On the polls . . .

ADAMAWA:

You mean to tell me that the people
Really apply foul means here when
We all should be teaming up together to
Work out the best to consolidate
This monument?

SOTIMO:

Adamawa, don't be so simple-minded.
Of course, the entire air is foul—
Foul. The air of politics is foul—
Foul, very foul, and it stinks through
And through. And it becomes fetid
When people aspire to grab it by all means.

OZOMA:

So the lesson to take home today is
That when merit is strangulated,

The air of power becomes fetid. And consumed
In large doses, it's so thick and toxic
That it chokes.

SOTIMO and OZOMA:

Ha! Ha! Ha! Ha!

ADAMAWA:

But it's tragic!

OZOMA:

Indeed, it's the death of us all.

ADAMAWA:

It's sad when merit ceases to
Be the measure.
This monument, so well contoured and
Carved, will crumble on us all.

OZOMA:

Ho! Ho! Ho! Why must you weep
Louder than the owner of the corpse?

SOTIMO:

That's no concern for the sons of the
Soil.

ADAMAWA:

But if they're truly sons of the soil,
Then they must fight to combat rust
In their woods. If they're sons of
The soil, they must stand to plant
The best! They hold forth a mirror
Of selfless effort as
To bare the monument, as everlasting
Edifice for the universe
For posterity to see with, and lean on,
It should be their pride.

SOTIMO:

That is an ideal.

OZOMA:

Indeed. But look around you. Where
Are your sons of the soil? Is it not
Always we, the strangers among them,
Who till, plow, mold the soil for
This monument that is their great claim?
Where are these so-called landowners
Who crumble the edifice in their own

Soil, waiting on strangers to
Mold from their sweat while they
Lie about for inheritance and
Anointment from the sweat of others?
Where are they? *(Enter* IYASE *and* IDEHEN *unnoticed)*

SOTIMO: *(sarcastically)*
Of course, somewhere scheming, meeting,
planning, intrigues on who to uproot,
Who to maim, how to install themselves
and reap where they sow not . . .
*(*IYASE *clears his throat. The workers are startled)*

IYASE: *(arrogantly)*
Of course, here we are!
We are the sons of the soil!
Do you doubt it?
(Silence. The workers look upon them in disgust)
Do you doubt it?
No, you dare not.

IDEHEN:
You can only pine in your labor
And jealousy.

IYASE:
Many are born to serve,
Many are born to sow.

IDEHEN:
For a few to reap.

IYASE:
Look! Our hands are golden,
These red feathers,
These soft palms are not products
Of cowries but of royal blood.

IDEHEN:
Till from season to season,
Plow from dawn to dusk,
Walk through seven seas and seven
Forests. Ours is timeless,
And no matter how much you till,
This monument belongs to us—to us,
And no power of yours can lift it
From our soil.

IYASE:

And your sweat will always irrigate
Our land.

OZOMA: *(No longer able to contain himself, addresses the other workers)*

Arise, friends!
Arise, I say!
The fowl must cease to feed into
The goat's stomach.
Arise, I say!
Let the dead bury their dead if
That is their wish.

ADAMAWA:

No, Ozoma! our sweat and our muscles
Molded the concrete for that monument
To this point. We must
Not hand it over to drunkards.
This land, this monument is great
Because our black hands
Made it so. The monument belongs to us too.

SOTIMO:

Those drunk on power that is yet to come—
(IYASE plucks the unripe orange. IDEHEN plucks one, too.)

IDEHEN: *(taunting the workers)*

Challenge us
If you can.

IYASE:

Ha! Ha! Ha! . . .
The election comes up one market
Day from now.

IDEHEN:

We shall see who the real owner of
The land is . . .

OZOMA and ADAMAWA:

We shall see!
(Blackout)

MOVEMENT THREE

Night in Idu. IYASE *creeps into the palace, looking with relish on the throne, the magnificence of the building and the surroundings. He performs some rites, sprinkling some potions and herbs as he chants incantations. Brief silence. He breaks the solemnity and goes into a wild reverie.*

IYASE:
Ah, the gods of Idu know that
I was born to rule.
If not, why on Earth did they starve
Ogiso, our last king, of an heir to
The throne?
And in the absence of a son
Ha! Ha! Ha! Ha!
A rope which creeps to the middle of the
Road knows that it will make a
Good mat for the passing foot.
The gods are truly wise.
I, Iyase, elected as the mouth
Of my dumb people. And they shall
Be my stool.
Though without wings,
I shall be the eagle,
And they shall patch me up—
And pluck out their flesh to
adorn me with feathers, for flight—
And for this favor
That I have undertaken to do them,
Their backs shall be the ferry which
I shall monkey—on to glory.
Their frames shall provide the
Platform for my transformation,
And their bare skins, soaked in
Sweat and blood, shall provide the
Carpet for my ascension to glory.
For this favor that I sign to do them,
I shall be their eagle,

And these stranger elements in our
Midst shall be the needle which sews
And sews but will never wear!
I, Iyase, shall be the eagle,
Though without wings,
They shall patch me up.
*(He touches the red feather on his head and begins to
smile)*
Or did they think I took this title
For amusement?
A bird with wings must fly and fly.
I must! Even against all wills,
Against all winds,
Against all currents,
Whether from within or from without.
The constitution says without an
Heir to the throne, the people
By consensus must elect a king-surrogate.
Not man but woman. Woman to sit as king
For three seasons. That is the constitution . . .
Constitution . . .
And we are the living interpreters of
The law of the land.
Tfia constitution!
If issues are solved by consensus—
Ah—these hordes of foreigners planted
Here and there might close our lot
In a downward swing
And I, Iyase, the head of my people.
Upright as the law may be,
We, I, Iyase with the royal blood of Idu,
Can *bend or break* the law,
And when I get to the top—
When I get to the top—
Shall swoop
Down on these strangers as things
Only fit for carrion.
*(At this point, he is becoming so agitated and hysterical
that he takes some steps briskly toward the throne. He
gets near, and, as if frightened, retreats but continues
to repeat to himself the last lines)*
And when I get to the top,

When I get to the top,
Like a hungry eagle with a swoop,
Scoop these stranger elements as
Carrion.
When I get to the top . . .
When I get to the top . . .
(He is still pacing up and down, but at the next lines, he gets so menacingly near to the throne, and just as he is about to sit and pose as king, ANEHE *breaks in on him)*
When I get to the top . . .
I, Iyase, shall
Bend the law . . .

ANEHE: *(interrupting)*
Or break
It, Iyase . . .
*(*IYASE *frightened that he has been discovered, makes a dash for the throat of* ANEHE, *but discovering who it is, stops. He is so shocked that his feet remain glued to the floor and his outstretched hands freeze in the air. His eyes look dilated and wild, and for some time he attempts to recover himself. Gradually he begins to calm down. Backing* ANEHE *partly in shame and partly in fear that she might reveal his secret, he breaks the silence)*

IYASE:
Anehe, what brings you here at this
Time of the night?

ANEHE:
With all due respect, I should be
Asking my lord that question.

IYASE: *(getting wild)*
You mean, I, as the Iyase, most prominent
Chief in this land, should not come to
Inspect the work our great king has
Left us to complete?

ANEHE:
Certainly not, my lord!
But honest men work from sunrise to
Sunset. Not when the night is half gone.
Iyase!
Night is for witches,
Schemers, and blood suckers.

IYASE: *(eyes looking wilder now, attempts to halt* ANEHE'S *mouth)*
Anehe! Stop, Anehe!!
(He approaches her, begins to calm down, looks straight into her eyes, holds her firmly in his arms)

IYASE:
Anehe, won't you like to live
Forever as a queen?

ANEHE:
Of course!
The taste of honey is friend
Everlasting to the tongue,
And once tasted,
The tongue enthralled flips as antennae
In search of more juices to savor.

IYASE:
Anehe, swear . . .
Swear to me your lips shall never
Speak of what your eyes saw tonight
Nor your ears ever heard.
And you will, I promise, remain
Cushioned in the bosom of power
When kingship makes me.

ANEHE: *(getting more seductive)*
You know I need not
Swear.
A bee is always lured by nectar.
My husband, the king, is gone.
If he loved me so much, why did he
Leave me here alone to bleed inside
Like a mature rubber tree ready
For the cutlass to open up to sap,
But no donor comes?
*(*IYASE *grabs her and embraces her firmly to his bosom and stops as suddenly as he started, to ask)*
Will you be true forever?

ANEHE:
True, I will.

IYASE:
Then go fetch me Idehen. Tell
Him that I await him here in the dark.
*(*ANEHE, *about to leave, takes a few steps, hesitates)*

ANEHE:

Eh . . . But one heavy thought
Weighs deep in my mind.

IYASE:

Open up, my petals.

ANEHE:

Eh—ehm . . . ehm . . .

IYASE:

Be quick lest the cock announce
Itself on us and stagger other people
From sleep to wake in earnest for
The dawn. Be quick.

ANEHE:

Come closer to me. The walls have
Wide ears. And this air of night,
Though as thick as the pod of oil
Bean seed, can disperse our thoughts
to the sun.
(IYASE *takes a step or two nearer*)

IYASE:

Now quick . . .

ANEHE:

It's Bia . . . the last queen of Ogiso.
You know she bears a child which any
Moment from now may arrive.
If this child is a boy,
Then . . .

IYASE: *(nodding his approval)*

Aha! My ambition,
Then my ambition
Is ruined!
(Pause)
We must take hold of her,
That pregnant fool!
That child must not live
As long as I live!

ANEHE:

So be it, my lord.

IYASE:

Now, go and tell Idehen
That Iyase is on his feet here

in expectancy . . .
Say he must see me at first cock-crow.

ANEHE:

Yes, my lord.
(Exit ANEHE *through the palace gates.* IYASE *stares long-ingly at the throne. He hears an unusual female voice and then takes to his heels. Queen* ZO *enters, looking worried as if she searches for something)*

ZO:

I thought I heard voices?
Voices deep in motive,
But here I come aroused
And only emptiness abound.
I can swear I heard voices . . .
*(*ANEHE *reenters)*

ANEHE: *(interrupting)*

You hear no voices, Zo.
*(*ZO *is startled)*
Only the echoes of desire and
Mischief.
Otherwise, how can a queen explain
Her mission to a throne sitting
Askance in this hour of night?
When fellows turn cockroach
They owe the kingdom a cogent
explanation!
What is your desire around the
Throne?

ZO:

Perhaps you believe you have
More claim to be here than I,
But note
A finger which exceeds downward
From the navel must state its
Mission.

ANEHE:

Perhaps it travels to quell
The turbulence within.

ZO:

I see—
But not one hand is endowed to
Stir up turbulence . . .

ANEHE: *(interrupting her)*
    To quell, I said . . .
    For now, go inside.
    This is no time for quibbles.
    Strong winds threaten
    To defile the monument,
    And I'm here to spearhead
    The direction.

ZO:
    Oh!
    Then it's a grave matter which
    We all must bear. I must come with
    You . . .

ANEHE: *(agitatedly)*
    No!

ZO:
    But why?
    The great king entrusted
    This monument to us all . . .

ANEHE: *(cajoling her)*
    My dear one,
    Queen though you are,
    Some of us have nerves
    Which cooked on heat
    Increase in strength,
    Some have strong will,
    Some frail, like yours . . .

ZO:
    No.
    The reed on shore may look frail
    But each tide and wind combing
    And bending it downward
    Still strengthens it to rise upward.

ANEHE:
    Hmm . . .
    All the same, I know your heart, Zo.
    Go inside.
    Certain tasks desire
    Discreet hands.
    Go inside,
    Wish me well.

ZO:

As you wish. Good night.

(Exit ANEHE. ZO *waits for* ANEHE *to depart. She is pensive, then she runs to* BIA *to alert her while her words can be heard disappearing with her. For a while the air reeks of mischief)*

Anehe, mother to none but to intrigue
And evil. Ah, the black goat must be
Driven to its pen early.
I must go unfold to Bia
What burdens my stomach.

(As she is about to leave, she hears footsteps, attempts to hide, but ANEHE *is there with* IYASE *and* IDEHEN *already)*

ANEHE:

There she goes.
Give charge to her feet.

*(*IYASE *throws a basket over her head. The males get hold of her. They bind her hands and feet, and although she struggles, they subdue her, and* IDEHEN *carries her away. A horrifying scream followed by a crashing noise. The echo of O-o-o-o-o-o-o can be heard)*

IYASE:

That is one obstacle gone.

ANEHE:

Now, the Queen B.

IYASE:

One strong smash on her belly
And she empties its contents
Like a pregnant spider under foot.
Bring her here!

ANEHE:

At your service, chief,
But Bia's load is
More than enough for ten generations
Of us.

IDEHEN: *(reentering)*

Go fetch Wa.

IYASE:

Can she be trusted?
She, too, is a foreign element like Zo . . .

IDEHEN:
What you must do is suck the orange,
And the pulp
You throw away.

ANEHE:
Well said.
The game of politics is divide and rule.

IDEHEN:
Divide and take.

IYASE:
Winner takes all.

ANEHE:
No argument!
Time is no friend of ours.
We must proceed.
(Exit ANEHE. *Returns shortly with* WA *and* BIA. BIA *is visibly frightened)*

IYASE:
Give her the potion.

WA: *(trying to caution them)*
Be careful!
We must not seem to be destroying
That which our king has planted.

IDEHEN:
Yes. And run the risk of the sharp
Tongue of these foreign bodies.

WA:
Bia is far gone in pregnancy.

ANEHE:
Let her be far gone in death.
We cannot fold our arms and have
Strangers overthrow us. Give
Her the potion.
*(*BIA *attempts to run away. They hold her firmly and blindfold her.* ANEHE *gives* WA *the thorny husks of a palm fruit bunch to hold)*

WA:
Well, the eyes of the entire
Kingdom are on us.
They who ride on others' backs
To pluck creepers on their paths

Must step down to feel the heat
On the ground. My hands quiver . . .
I cannot go on.

IYASE:
Do my bidding.

WA:
Why should I?

IYASE:
I command it!

WA: *(hesitates, then replies)*
Your command reveals
My bearing.
I accept, feet wobbling,
Fledgling in obedience, but firmly
In search of bearing. I accept.

IYASE: *(aside to* IDEHEN*)*
This Queen Wa,
I am not sure of her.

IDEHEN:
Me, too. Her tongue as sharp as cutlass.

IYASE:
We will take care of her.

WA:
As you wish, Your Majesty.

IYASE:
Idehen, we must leave.
Even the handling of blood has
Its own art, and in such bloody chores
Are females better than males.
We must leave it to them.
*(*ANEHE *and* WA *try to force* BIA *into a porch by the throne
as she resists)*

BIA:
What is my offense?

WA:
My dear Queen B,
Even the best of us at the best
Of times is a toy in the hands
Of power and men.

BIA: *(muffled but audible)*
The gods take charge of
Those who climb to the top by cutting

Down others on their path . . .
And though you will my anguish and
Loss, the gods sleep not!

IDEHEN:

But that child you bear must sleep.
Remember the story of Agbonor and
Kolanut trees which look like twins.

BIA:

Though the Agbonor tree was cut down
To avenge the death of the kola tree,
When kola died
Agbonor produced new branches.
What will be will be . . .

IYASE:

She takes liberty of our kindness.
(to WA*)*
Force her in! *(They subdue* BIA *and push her into the
porch. The women disappear into the porch. As soon as*
ANEHE *gets hold of* BIA, WA *flees from the opposite
direction)*

ANEHE:

Will you hold her firmly now?
Wa, hold her! *(She looks around;* WA *is gone.* BIA *struggles, but* ANEHE *soon subdues her.* IYASE *and* IDEHEN *pace
anxiously. Drum and xylophone echo the agitation in
the background as the chiefs await the outcome of their
intrigue. Soon the cock crows, punctuated by the
rhythm of the drum and the shrill cry of the newborn.*
ANEHE *lifts a husk of palm fruit and places it on the feet
of* BIA. ANEHE *rushes out bearing a baby in a mat)*

IYASE and IDEHEN: *(betraying their anxiety)*

What sex?
*(*ANEHE *is in such a hurry that she does not stop to an-
swer.* IYASE *and* IDEHEN *rush in)*
What sex?

BIA:

A male.

IDEHEN:

Shut up! Shameless slut! Who says
You have a human child? Is that not
A husk of palm fruit between your thighs?

BIA: *(sobbing)*
But . . . but . . . it's a male. Anehe
is gone with it . . .

IDEHEN: *(threateningly)*
Shut up! Or we shall shut you up
For the last time.
(BIA *still sobbing*)

IYASE: *(aside to* IDEHEN*)*
Anehe has gone with the child
To ensure that it makes good
Meal for rodents on the bush path.
(IYASE, *relieved and confident, speaks to*
IDEHEN*)* That tree planted by Ogiso
To stand between us and the throne
Must be uprooted.

IDEHEN:
And has indeed been uprooted.
Ha! Ha! Ha! *(They salute each other)*

BIA:
The yam tuber rots and is buried forever . . .
In the tail but with head, it soon sprouts anew.

IYASE:
Bia, you are a dreamer. The yam that must be
Planted is cut to pieces first . . .

BIA:
Even if it be just a very slight piece,
So long as it is a head,
It can sprout to full length.

IYASE:
Indeed, they have always called you
Senseless. But not until this moment
Could I ever be sure that you were.
If you could not bear a male, why at
Least could you not bear a female
And here you are with an empty husk.

IDEHEN:
See what empty fruit you bear?

BIA:
I could swear I heard the cry of a male child.

IYASE:
You lie!

IDEHEN:

You lie!

BIA:

No! You cannot blindfold me forever!

(She pulls off the cloth ANEHE *has tied around her eyes)*

IYASE: *(suddenly emerging)*

Now shut up your big mouth and remain

Forever silent!

BIA: *(startled, silent)*

You may decree the final word,

But the gods execute . . . *(She begins to sob once again)*

The gods sleep not.

*(*ANEHE *entering)*

ANEHE:

Indeed the gods are wise . . .

IYASE:

Any problem?

ANEHE: *(panting)*

I heard footsteps and voices

Along the pathway not far from here.

IYASE: *(anxiously)*

And your burden?

My fingers went to task

Immediately on its throat.

My duty to the throne

I have executed

To preserve us,

And here I am.

(She shows her bloody palm. IYASE *and* IDEHEN *jubilate. But soon the voices and footsteps are more audible and visible. Two females, one old, one young. It is Queen* ZO *and her ancient mother from across the waters.* ZO *is now disguised as a very young female called Wazobia.* ZO *should be made up to look about twenty years old. The* OLD TERMITE *is blind)*

ANEHE:

They are near.

*(*ANEHE, IDEHEN, *and* IYASE *flee)*

OLD TERMITE:

Wazobia, my child. The air is so thick

and dense, you can touch it.

(She feels with her palms)
It's so thick you can cut it. Can't you smell it?

ZO:

It is the thick air of the clouds,
Heavy, humid, and dark as the harbinger of
An impending rain. But it's only the
thick touch of night visiting . . .

OLD TERMITE:

And it is to this dense and choking air
You wish to return?

ZO:

Mother. I love you, Mother. But I
Long to return to roots all the same. Idu
Nurses the worms that consume her own
Children. You fled from Idu. Having smelled
The foul air so early. I, too, have fled like
Many others. How much longer must we cower
In the face of evil? The air that is hot gives
Way for the air that is cool. Is that not the
Natural state of things?
Why must we forever strive to accept the
    imbalance?

OLD TERMITE:

Because fighting it sometimes leaves us bathing in ashes,
Each new heat departs leaving its own trail of sweat.
Each new world hangs on a balance.
Wazobia, the wind, too, is strong, my child.

ZO:

That is my life. We must balance that which lies pre-
    cariously
On its head or it will tip over, leaving us subdued.
We must strive to shoulder it.

OLD TERMITE: *(elated)*

That is it, my child! Shoulder it, not head it, lest our
Heads be cracked in the process . . .
*(ZO seeing the baby by the footpath,
shows it to the* OLD TERMITE*)*

ZO:

Look, Mother!

OLD TERMITE:

What?

ZO:

Look!

OLD TERMITE:

You know my eyes see not things hidden nor
Facts wrapped up.

ZO:

I know that. Even then, blind though
You are, you found me hanging loose
On that branch of a tree.

OLD TERMITE:

Even then, my child, I never saw you. I only
Heard your cry for deliverance. I was groping
Just only for wood for my herbs.

ZO:

And I am the wood
That will give fire to the kingdom's herbs
To enkindle light in this dark abyss.

OLD TERMITE:

That is my daughter! My woman of tomorrow!
I found you all the same. You, the pillar
To hold forth an aging frame. The wood to give
Warmth to this cold kingdom.

ZO:

Ah, Mother! You have forgotten so soon. A
moment ago, the air was so warm and thick you
Could cut it.

OLD TERMITE:

Yes, cut it. What else is expected of one
Who seeks?

ZO: *(laughing)*

Mother, you are deep like the
Earth herself.
Cut the air to purge it of excess,
Then lighten it and inflate it again.

OLD TERMITE: *(amused)*

Wazobia! Remember I cannot see
Facts wrapped up . . .

ZO:

However knitted they are, we must
Then untie . . .

OLD TERMITE:

Show me that which you see. Perhaps,
For once, through your eyes, we all
May see . . .

ZO:

A male child, strong-limbed, mangled,
And thrown by the wayside
And left to the mercy of hungry wolves.

OLD TERMITE:

Ah—world!
A black male child costly as a gem,
And I who longed for one since I
Lost my twins to the slave raiders, to be
Blessed with a male child? He
Will give me joy for the rest of my
Ebbing life. He shall begin the era
Of glory.

ZO:

Now, can you see the value of your
Leading me back to our kingdom
To give aid in the selection of our
king-surrogate?
My feet point to the east . . .

OLD TERMITE: *(excitedly)*

Now I can see how the gods
Reward the selfless.
Your name was Zo.

ZO:

You called me Wa-zo-bia instead.
The world is one and whole,
Except men try to cut it to fragments.
The task of woman is to build—to create.
Let us return home,
Let this child lead our life . . .
(Excited and smiling broadly, OLD TERMITE *takes up the child to her bosom. The child emits a wild, anguished cry, and stops. Silence.* ZO *looks intently at the child and bursts out again)*

OLD TERMITE: *(muttering)*

Always!
Hope ever seems to sprout,

But take root it will not. *(She gets hysterical)*
Oh! This generation of termites!
With one hand uprooting,
With another burying,
And soon hurrying to mold
Anew from self-made debris.
Do we ever learn? *(Brief silence)*
Do we ever learn?
Do we ever, ever . . . ever . . .

ZO: *(tenderly to* OLD TERMITE*)*
Learn for life. Remember, Mother,
We live in twin-fold of life and death.
Henceforth
Celebrate my homecoming,
Take the child with you.
Return, Mother,
Return *(Pause, exit* OLD TERMITE *with the child. Brief si-
lence.* ZO, *more resolved, bursts out)*
Female though I am, aroused to celebrate my home-
    coming,
Celebrate my inheritance of breath
To male lost.
I, Wazobia,
Native to this soil,
Must sprout from its ferment.
The oil bean pod which dangles
And explodes may land sullen.
It also
Swells to form two lobes
Which once parted and smiling
Thrust forth tongues of sprouting hymen
Or more likely
Elongating and penetrating
The womb of time, drop the lobes
Dangling the testicles of the
Gender of a generation.
My feet point to the east . . .
My feet feel the antennae of the sun . . .
(Cock-crow. BIA, *tired but agitated, emerges alone from
the palace. She is searching frantically and muttering
to herself.* ZO *approaches, hears her voice and stops)*

BIA: *(tearfully singing about her child)*
I swear I could swear
I heard the sound of a male child . . .
A male voice, strong and firm . . .
But here I am,
Left with this husk and thorn,
Thrusting forth a bosom sore with milk . . .
(At this point ZO *enters.* BIA, *startled and thinking that* ANEHE *and her gang have come to kill her, shouts)*
Please, spare . . . !
*(*BIA *shivers but soon realizes it is not the expected ene-mies.* ZO, *surprised, stops. Pause. Not getting any re-sponse from* ZO, BIA *asks)*
Be mild in your task. I am just a
Helpless victim. The male who
Would have been my backbone they
Have just crushed.

ZO:
A male
Did you say?

BIA:
A child, my child . . . *(She gasps, trying hard to block the cascading tears)*

ZO:
What happened to him?

BIA:
I could swear I heard his cry, but
Those who fear I might produce
A male child for the throne forced
Him out of me and . . . and . . . and . . . ah . . .
(She breaks down in tears)

ZO: *(This rings a bell to her, but she is determined not to divulge her secret. Brief silence)*
Hmm . . . Well, sense what you feel . . . blood,
But don't mind.
Men plot, but the gods execute,
The gods do not sleep.

BIA: *(encouraged)*
Who are you?

ZO:
Does it really matter who I am? I am just a wayfarer.
Wa-zo-bia. Call me Wazobia.

BIA:

But you must have a name.

ZO:

A name? A name . . .
What's in a name?
We wear names and
Change them.
Names too like clothes get worn out.
Sometimes they get threadbare,
But we wear them all the same
Hoping to patch them together.
Well, why am I saying
All this anyway?
All you wish to know is what people call me.
Wa-zo-bia.

BIA:

Wa-zo-bia?

ZO:

Yes.

BIA: *(excitedly)*

Oh, Wazobia!
That name chimes in my ears
Like . . . like . . . like
a home call.
Oh, Zo—Wazobia!
A stranger and yet a friend!
Will you take me with you?
My name is Queen Bia. Harnessed
to the chariots of the last king,
But since he's gone
They've turned me to their footmat.
Please, please, please, Wazobia,
Take me back home with you.

ZO:

There's that in your voice which
forms like a blood knot.
We must come together. That is the meaning of my name:
    Wa-zo-bia—
Come, come, come together!

BIA:

In that short name you have knitted all the
Threads together. Here in this term

Where the seams stare loosely,
Reaching out for a tender arm
To tuck them in and give
The world a form. We once had a Zo
And Wa in this palace . . .

ZO:

Well, worries are interior to feeling. My tongue
Is heavy now. I choose not to speak,
For as the elders say,
There will be enough sleep for the dead one in
The grave.
Don't you see vision of us all converge here?
I was born to this kingdom
Our body branded with hot coals and
scattered to pieces by oppressors
For those left, the search for survival and freedom has
scattered us.
As a daughter of the kingdom and
In obedience to the constitution,
I have come to cast my lot.
The tree stump hewn and thrown by the
wayside can sprout anew . . .
Soon sprouts anew . . . will sprout anew.
When a king passes, trees around
the palace are hewn down in anticipation
Of growth from nodes that branch out.
Which node becomes dominant, no one knows. But I
Have come to cast my lot as custom demands on
daughters of Idu.
We must elect the king-surrogate
Whose bearing shall give us direction.

BIA:

Oh, you've come for the election?
I hear it's at hand.

ZO:

Yes. The third cock-crow will
Announce it.
For now, please shelter me and
This hand shall be your support
And this back shall be your bone.
The gods sleep not . . .

BIA:

So it would seem. *(Light fades into the next)*

MOVEMENT FOUR

Time is just before dawn. IYASE, *alone, darting from one side of the village square to the throne, relishing his new position as the heir-apparent*

IYASE:

The oil bean pod has exploded,
The seed lost, Iyase gathers
At the swollen foot of the hill.
Ah!
There sits the throne,
Naked like a woman undressed,
And will it be said
That I, Iyase,
Stallion that I am,
Dared not thrust forth
This manhood poised
Whether she bears it or not . . .?
In the relay of semen,
Many though the companions
Or competitions may seem
Or seem to be,
One, only one, just one,
Must the virgin-egg lap,
And these friends of time
In time be paid off
As laborers . . .

ANEHE:

There he is!
(IYASE, *embarrassed but trying to cover up, pauses. Enter* ANEHE *and* IDEHEN)

IYASE: *(stammering)*

Ah . . . em . . . ehn . . .

IDEHEN:

Iyase,
You disappoint us,
Wearing this kind of shroud of inaction about
To cripple us all.

ANEHE: *(taunting)*

Perhaps he longs
For what he's lost in Bia.
You have an eye for her,
Don't you?

IYASE: *(regaining his composure)*

How can?

IDEHEN:

Man,
Pull your loins together,
Gird them for the tasks ahead.

ANEHE:

Time for king-surrogate.

IYASE:

Ah—
Time to yarn.

IDEHEN:

Beat the gong!
That the deaf ears of the
Wall may open.

IYASE:

Indeed!
That the great pods may split
For growth.
Idehen!
Borrow the spirit of a hare
To the sons and daughters of our soil,
Bring them to those grounds,
Give voice to our summons
And to our plans. Silence.
(Exit IDEHEN. IYASE *and* ANEHE, *now alone, exchange know-ing glances.* ANEHE, *looking lustful, captures* IYASE's *eyes which seem to be wandering far away. Silence)*

ANEHE: *(breaking the silence)*

With the hare laid off,
What plots the fox for a hen?

IYASE:

Maize . . .

ANEHE:

And Idehen?

IYASE:

A mere hunting dog
Easily entertained
With mashed yam in palm oil
And offal.

ANEHE:

But his ambition reeks and swells
Around the throne.

IYASE:

Oh, let him dream.
You cannot stop them dreaming.
Let him dream.
Soon reality punctures the reservoir
Of desire.

ANEHE:

To wake them up?

IYASE:

To drown them.

ANEHE:

And crown us!

IYASE:

Ah . . .

(They hold and regard each other tenderly. In the distance, flute plays)

IYASE:

I hear the distant calls of service.

ANEHE:

Of desire . . . ?

*(*IDEHEN *arrives suddenly. The couple, startled, disengages)*

IYASE:

Oh, you are back already?

IDEHEN:

And ready.
The kingdom awaits us.

(Light dims and lingers on until there is a slow and flickering transition into the next scene, and then a steady growth of light)

MOVEMENT FIVE

The village square. Time is just before dawn. IYASE, IDEHEN, *and* ANEHE, *looking victorious, assemble all daughters and sons of the soil who live within the kingdom. They hold a secret meeting. The air is full of excitement.*

IYASE:
With the ground cleared,
Sons and daughters of the soil,
It is time for selection of grain
To separate yam from cassava. In this
Our vote must form a solid block,
Each one to bury the hatchet against
His brother, for anger between brothers
Goes not beyond skin deep.
When brothers fight, they leave
Strangers to share their kingdom.

IDEHEN:
Your vote must be one.
*(*CHORUS *of sons and daughters raise their hands in unison)*

CHORUS:
With one breath
Our force we bind.
*(*ANEHE *pushes forward her own daughters,* IYASE*'s and* IDEHEN*'s. The princesses form a half-moon while the rest are still in a full-moon shape around them)*

ANEHE: *(pointing to the inner circle)*
Sons and daughters
Of the soil. Swear, swear that this must
Be your vote.
And whoever divulges our secret or
Goes against us shall give his head as toll.

CHORUS:

We swear!

(ANEHE sprinkles water of the bond between them. They alternate their half-moon and full-moon formation three times. The xylophone takes up the rhythm of their excitement which is soon subdued by the TOWN CRIER's gong and voice as he summons the kingdom to wake up into a new dawn of decision at the square)

TOWN CRIER:

Termites of Idu,

Today is the market day

For the election of our surrogate

King from among daughters of the land.

Each one to cast vote.

(The present assembly is soon swelled by the number of termites in the territory. Other termites begin to assemble. The first batch is made up mostly of commoners. IYASE, IDEHEN, and ANEHE leave to rejoin them later)

FIRST COMMONER:

It is a shame,

Termites locking horns in

Their territory.

SECOND COMMONER:

I hear they are making it

Exclusive vote.

THIRD COMMONER:

Hmm. That's where they go wrong.

FIRST COMMONER:

Why is it only time to harvest

That the yield is made exclusive?

Have we not together tended

The plants?

THIRD COMMONER:

We mold mountains

Even from the waste of men, and

We, the downtrodden,

Make roads from rocky pathways

Where others have failed.

SECOND COMMONER:

The whole world is a passage:

While some ride free on the

Backs of others,

Others trudge on through and
Through to the end.

FIRST COMMONER:

Worms have so infested our
Soil that even Ozoma said to Sotimo
yesterday, "If these people shake
your hands, count your fingers thereafter."

(At this point, OZOMA, ADAMAWA, *and* SOTIMO *arrive. Soon
the number swells with the arrival of* IYASE *and* IDEHEN.
*The congregation rises to register its respect to these
chiefs. Slow music in the background, but as soon as
the chiefs arrive, music increases in tempo until* IYASE
stops it)

IYASE: *(clearing his throat)*

Idu!

CHORUS: *(faintly)*

Eh.

IYASE: *(more forcefully)*

Idu!

CHORUS: *(still faintly)*

Eh.

IYASE: *(thunderously)*

Idu, are you not
All with me?

CHORUS: *(forcefully)*

Eh!

IYASE: *(reassured)*

It is now time for selection
Of seed.
One of our blood daughters to
Sit there in communion with
The gods until an heir is found
To the throne.
As a believer in hard-core
Tradition, I must warn that only
A daughter . . .
Only a daughter of this
Soil can be voted . . .

OZOMA:

Iyase, you lie!
Soil is soil east or west,
North or south . . .

IDEHEN: *(interrupting)*
No, Ozoma!
Soil is not soil.
Some are sandy,
Some are rocky,
Some are fertile,
Some are sterile.

IYASE:
Some red
And some brown.
That is why even the land
Is divided north or south,
east or west.

ADAMAWA:
Then, if such discrete
Divisions exist,
What is this kangaroo
Democracy that you manipulate
By which you call us all together
Only to split us and stress to us
How some of us are less than ants?

ADAMAWA:
The fowl must cease to feed into
The goat's stomach!
(Exit IYASE, IDEHEN, *and* ANEHE. *They hold secret talk)*

SOTIMO:
Split the franchise and
Split the kingdom.

OZOMA:
That shouldn't surprise you,
The game of politics is
Divide and rule.

ADAMAWA:
Divide and take.

SOTIMO:
Winner takes all.

CHORUS: *(of the younger termites)*
Winner takes all,
Winner takes all,
Winner takes all,
Winner—winner—winner—
Winner—takes all!

OZOMA:

This is a free society.
This monument belongs to
All of us.
The fact that it is seated in your
Backyard does not give you
Exclusive right of ownership . . .
(Reenter IYASE, IDEHEN, *and* ANEHE*)*

IYASE:

Indeed, rhetoric . . .
Rhetorics, Ozoma.
The gods are wise
When they create certain
Plains forests and others deserts!
What is before us is ours.

ADAMAWA and SOTIMO:

And ours, too,

IYASE:

A million generations of you.
Cannot equal
Any royal blood.

OZOMA:

Then we will not vote!

ADAMAWA:

It's their plot.

SOTIMO:

Let us go.
(The crowd, especially commoners, rises to leave when IYASE *calls them all to order again.* ANEHE *goes to whisper to him. They pull aside, invite* IDEHEN, *and confer briefly)*

IYASE: *(smiling mischievously)*
Termites! Termites!
Termites of Idu,
We have heard your petition.
The king who speaks not
The voice of his people
Makes himself an easy prey to their nails.
Idu, do I speak your minds?

CHORUS:

Eh!

IYASE:

That what we have started does
Not cave in on us,
We shall appoint from among us a
King-surrogate.

OZOMA: *(more irritated)*

No!

CHORUS:

No! No! No!

IDEHEN:

Idu!
Sit, "No,"
Stand, "No,"
Run, "No."
Ha ha! Why have we suddenly
Turned to toddlers learning
To speak for the first time
And the only answer to every
Issue is "No"?
Why, Idu?

ADAMAWA:

Ask your inner circles
That question,
You who sleep through the day
And turn owls at night!

IYASE:

One last chance,
Since elections have lost
Their value.

SOTIMO:

Correction! Not lost value
But lack merit in these parts.

IYASE:

As you please! Since we cannot vote,
Let us cast lots.

OZOMA:

Yes!
The gods do not sleep,
Let the gods decide.
(IYASE picks some gourd or small calabash)

IYASE:

A child. We need a child whose
Innocence shall bear us out
Of this rot . . .

(ANEHE and IDEHEN are now busy briefing their predicted candidates to cluster together so that luck will fall on at least one of the chosen candidates. In the process, they displace other candidates, including ZO. ZO and the other nonfavorite daughters are placed at the periphery in the background. Slow rhythm of xylophone accompanies the selection scene, but when the child is called in to bear the calabash, music increases to a crescendo. Then the calabash is thrown up. Music stops abruptly when it lands on the lucky candidate. There is general excitement. The child is brought in. ANEHE, IDEHEN, and IYASE keep winking at the child to direct the gourd at the marked area. Some rites are performed on the child, who also is given a potion to drink. Child takes up the gourd, takes three steps forward, three steps backward as instructed, dances (accompanied by music), and throws the calabash with general cry of excitement. The calabash crash-lands on an individual. It is ZO)

IDEHEN: *(befuddled)*

Ah!

ANEHE: *(stung)*

Wa?

IYASE: *(gasps)*

Zo?

CHORUS:

Wa-zo-bia!
Wazobia! Wazobia! Wazobia!

(Echo of "Wazobia" fills the air. Silence. The jubilation. Dance, music. The whole community is aflutter. IYASE, IDEHEN, and ANEHE, who are noticeably disappointed, soon join in the dance. ZO holds the staff of office, the calabash of life)

IDEHEN:

Ah!

ANEHE:

Wa?

IDEHEN:
  Zo?

ANEHE:
  Bia.

CHORUS: *(chanting)*
  Wa-zo-bia!
  Wa-zo-bia!
  Wa-zo-bia!

FIRST COMMONER:
  Wa-a-a!

SECOND COMMONER:
  Zo-o-o-o-o!

THIRD COMMONER:
  Bia-a-a-a!

CHORUS:
  Wa-zo-bia!
  Wa-zo-bia!
  Wa-zo-bia!

(A burst of music and dance. The whole community is aflutter, then sudden silence. IYASE, IDEHEN, *and* ANEHE, *though at first disappointed, soon join in the general excitement. The rites of coronation begin.* ZO *holds the staff of office, the adah (a golden spear). She stands in her fullness and majestic height, bearing the calabash up, down, three times. They are stunned by the revelation.* ANEHE *slumps. But the other members of the kingdom in their innocence continue their dance, undisturbed. All the chiefs must crown the new "king."* OZOMA, ADAMAWA, *and* SOTIMO *show obvious signs of happiness. So does* BIA. IYASE *and* IDEHEN *are still glued to one spot. The flurry of music continues.* ZO *now seated on her throne as king. Termites begin the coronation. The oldest termite takes three steps backward, takes up* ZO's *hands, and places them squarely on the arms of the throne. He takes up the crown and sets it on her head. In a very colorful ceremony,* ZO *is crowned king-surrogate by all the chief termites. Her regalia is that of the former king which gives her a masculine look, and she, too, strives as she adjusts herself to look like the former king. As she is being crowned, each subject dances in turn, some in groups kneel at her feet and*

dash home to produce gifts with which to pay their new king homage. The coronation over, the king-surrogate in the fullness of her regalia and majesty, bearing her height and role, stands as an imposing statue, then slowly begins to unmask herself as Queen ZO. IYASE *is the first to notice, the* ANEHE *and* IDEHEN. ANEHE *slumps immediately.* IYASE *and* IDEHEN, *shocked, stop. The king, now looking fiercely and intently at* IDEHEN, *lifts her adah higher up, first with both hands, then resting it solely in her right hand, pointing downward with her left. Total hush in the crowd. Music stops. The attention is now divided between the dissident chiefs,* IDEHEN *and* IYASE *on the one hand, and the king on the other.* IDEHEN, *confused, torn between the angry look of the crowd and the deadly smile of the king with the staff of office, surrenders, kneeling in total submission. One drum accolade accompanies* IDEHEN'S *submission, followed again by a potent silence, for* IYASE *still stands, eyes red, muscles taut like those of a wounded lion. The king-surrogate again lifts her burden with her adah first upward and gradually balancing it on her head returns it and, standing arms akimbo, instructs* IYASE)

ZO: *(pointing at* IYASE)
You will wash
My feet, Iyase!
*(*IYASE *does not obey but glares at her in disgust)*

ZO: *(steadily but authoritatively)*
Iyase,
on *my* feet!
*(*IYASE *still adamant.* ZO *slowly moves the adah downward as if to break it at the foot of* IYASE. *The crowd turns to mob* IYASE, *shouting, "Down, down, down!"* ZO *says, "Kneel." Like an animal trapped by an angry crowd,* IYASE *looks from face to face hoping for sympathy, but none is forthcoming. The crowd still continues to echo, "Down, Iyase, Iyase, down.")*

CHORUS:
The king is an Iroko.
No tree stands higher than the towering
Iroko. Down, Iyase! Down!
No one is greater than the kingdom.
(All the crowd is poised to charge at him in case he at-

tempts to run away. IYASE *takes three steps backward in resignation, kneels, face downward. The king-surrogate sits on the throne. The oldest chief offers her water in a gourd.* IYASE *advances, still kneeling, and begins to wash the feet of the king-surrogate.* ZO *stands. The crowd kneels immediately in submission. She steps forward, takes a royal dance step)*

ADAMAWA: *(pointing the direction to* ZO*)*
There
Are paths for kings,
This is our path.

ZO: *(dancing)*
No! I am woman! I carve my
Own path.
Termites of Idu,
A female leads you in
The new dance step. Up!
Lift your hands to the horizon.
A woman leads.
The future is in our hands.
Reach out together and pluck
The fruits you sow in this garden,
Together,
Reach out . . .
(Spotlight follows ZO *in her new direction. The drums throb, linger, house lights)*

The Reign of Wazobia

CAST

WAZOBIA: *King-surrogate or regent of Ilaaa in Anioma kingdom*

KAANEBI: *Her mother, later queen mother*

ANEHE:
WA:
ZO: } *The late king's wives, later Wazobia's queens or wives*
BIA:

OMU: *The female "King"*

IYASE: *Male chief*

IDEHEN: *Male chief*

OZOMA: *Male chief*

PRIEST OF ANI: *Custodian of the shrines and devotee of the Earth Goddess*

PRIEST OF OHENE: *Custodian of the shrines and devotee of the River Goddess*

MAN *(Also plays the role of* DRUMMER *and* TOWN CRIER*)*

WOMAN

CHORUS OF ILAAA: *Availability of cast will determine the number of chorus members. (The maidens, drummers, dancers,* MAN, WOMAN, *and even* KAANEBI *can be drawn from this group to minimize the number of cast members.)*

PROLOGUE

Anioma kingdom. It is night, but the moon slowly tears through the clouds, perforating the sky to expose the bare beauty and essence of this pastoral kingdom. As if to reveal more and in detail, the moon races beyond the clouds and finally gathers momentum to converge a pool of light focused at the center of Anioma kingdom. At this center is an empty throne with an effigy of the late king (Obi-ogiso) sitting side by side, and WA-ZOBIA in an outfit similar to that of the late king. She stands equidistant from the palace throne and the surrounding huts making up the community. We may call this portion right in front of the throne where WAZOBIA stands the village square which comprises the shrines, containing the ikenga[1] and ofor,[2] the king's meeting ground with the ancestors and market square for his people.

At the extreme right of this village square thus revealed is the stump of an iroko tree symbolically beheaded as if it is a flag flying at half-staff in recognition of the stature of the late king. In the background, a flute plays somber tunes which rise in crescendo until

---

[1] **Ikenga** and [2]**Ofor:** Wooden staff and shrine signifying manhood, great achievements, and symbolic link between the dead ancestors and the living.

overtaken by the vibrant rhythm of drums. At the center of this hot dance is WAZOBIA *surrounded by dancing women.* WAZOBIA *is at first adamant until a masquerade[3] plunges into the dance from nowhere, smiling, showing dance steps done backward, and the women thus compelled to join in the backward dance.* WAZOBIA *tries a step or two, stops abruptly, changes her step as if shaking off from the hypnotic backward dance of the masquerade. The women are prostrate, but the masquerade, angry, stops dancing abruptly, and the drumming ceases immediately. Exit masquerade with severe warning glare at* WAZOBIA *and the women. In the background, voices of women chant "Wazobia! Wazobia!! Wazobia!!!"* WAZOBIA, *at first shaken but soon regaining her confidence, orders the women to stand from their state of submission.*

WAZOBIA:
Arise, women!
They say your feet are feeble,
Show them those feet carry the burden of the womb.
They say your hands are frail,
Show them those hands have claws,
Show them those hands are heavy.
Wake up, women!
Arise, women!
Barricade the entrance to the city.
I can hear trumpet sounds,
Voices of men spitting blood to drown us.
With your claws hook them,
But spill no blood, for these are sons of our wombs.
(As WAZOBIA *makes these pronouncements, the women strip themselves almost naked as a sign of revolt. Women line the palace walls in ambush for the incursionists while* WAZOBIA *stands at the center of the palace square poised for action. More trumpets. The legion of men enters. Leading them are the chiefs with the* IYASE *thrusting forth a steaming pot with burning herbs which he presents to* WAZOBIA*)*

---

[3] **Masquerade:** A symbol of dead ancestors.

MOB OF MEN:
A present, Wazobia.

IYASE: *(solemnly)*
A present, Wazobia,
From the people
To end your reign of terror.

IDEHEN:
Accept, Wazobia!
The people demand!
(WAZOBIA, *at first serious and taut, thaws into a smile and, with swift sudden change, blares orders*)

WAZOBIA:
Arise, women!
The tigers are here!

MOVEMENT ONE

(At once, the women charge, forcing the hot pot of herbs to break on IYASE's feet. What happens here must appear like mock battle. Care should be taken to ensure that the movements are choreographed appropriately for greater effect. Sudden blackout, followed immediately by lights transposed to the next scene. WAZOBIA is alone)

WAZOBIA:
Ha ha ha ha a a a a!!
For three seasons Wazobia has reigned.
Three seasons, just *three* seasons,
And men are sweating in their anuses.
Three seasons!!!
That is their maximum for any female regent,
Interregnum like military intervention,
But I have known military intervention
Last 10, 15, . . . 20 years!!!
I have only intervened here three seasons,
Only three seasons wiping their nose,
Cleaning their tears,

And now they want me to step down.
Should I or
Should I not?
(She weighs the question awhile)
So they want Wazobia to step down
So they can rig . . . elect a male king.
Should I or
Should I not?
Perhaps I should . . .
It's the voice of the people . . . the
People . . . people . . .
(suddenly changing her mind and becoming resolute)
But whose people?
Why should I?
A hen at midterm,
On my lap they threw the throne.
Should I lap it?
(wavering again)
Should I not?
But it's time to go . . .
It's not that easy to go . . .
It's not easy to leave . . .
Power, like crack,
Once injected turns you gay,
But it, too, can crack your skull,
And because they believe
Women carry pulp heads,
They administer power to them
In infantile aliquots
Ha! Ha! Ha!
Women . . . infants?
I, Wazobia,
Will show them
That women bear elephant tusks
Over their shoulders
Ha ha ha ha a a a a . . .
*(Her attendant drummer, thinking she calls for him,
stampedes on her)*

DRUMMER:
Here, my king . . .
*(He suddenly realizes that his king is in a rather un-
usual state of mind. Her eyes are fiery. He stands be-*

mused and confused, then attempts to retreat, but WA-
ZOBIA *has her eyes fixed like binoculars on him. Like a
panther, she pounces on him, grabs him with both
hands, shakes him as one would shake a pear tree
laden with ripe fruit)*

WAZOBIA:
They want Wazobia down.
Should I or should I not?

DRUMMER: *(stultified)*
Em . . . yea . . . no . . . yea! No! No! My king . . .
*(*WAZOBIA, *as if satisfied, relaxes her hold on him and lets
him fall. She suddenly becomes frantic again)*

WAZOBIA:
Drum, drum, drum for me.
I shall dance from Kaduna to Kaura Namoda.
Drum, drum, drum.
I, Wazobia, *am* anwulinwu,[4]
Stuck unto the body and soul of this clan!
(The DRUMMER *obeys while she does a frenetic jig, but
suddenly* WAZOBIA *stops dancing, and the* DRUMMER *halts,
confused; pause, each staring the other in the face)*

WAZOBIA: *(pounding her chest)*
I, Wazobia,
Am the masquerade
Who dances the hot steps of the new day,
The finger which laps the soup
When it is hottest
While the men scrape it from the sides,
The lead masquerade who
Speaks many tongues.
I, the masquerade
Whose feet imprint
New images on the sagging face
Of this land without a father.
I, Wazobia, whose . . . whose . . .
(She suddenly turns angrily to the DRUMMER)
What are you waiting for?
Sing, sing my praise.
That is what you are paid to do . . .

---

[4] **Anwulinwu:** Feathery, prickly, sticky thorns on okra for cooking soup.

(The DRUMMER *takes up the cue, drumming, at first falter-*
ing, but soon he gains mastery. While he drums, singing
her praises, WAZOBIA *relishes it, begins to spray him with*
wads of currency notes)

DRUMMER:
May your reign outlast you,
The masquerade who stands, nose down,
While others sniff head high in the sky.
Wazobia, whose hands mend the tattered
Sinews of our world!

WAZOBIA: *(interrupting him)*
Inflicted for ages by your men
Who ruled—misruled—us,
Leaving the world in tatters.
Sing, drum, drum, drum, and I will dance
From Kaduna to Kaura Namoda.
I, Wazobia, have come with these feminine
Fingers to embroider it,
To knit your world together. Accept,
Men, men accept.
But no! They have come again!!!
They want Wazobia ousted.
Men refuse, for it is only fight and
Plunder they know.
When, when, when will men learn to
Accept that they cannot gain peace from war?
When will men accept their redeemers?
They want Wazobia ousted.
Wazobia, too, resists and will persist.
I, Wazobia, will show them
What the left hand did to the anus.
I am the Earth itself.
Where will you move it to?
I, Wazobia, have tasted power and *will not go.*
*(*WAZOBIA *is interrupted by female singers and dancers*
jubilating to the palace to pay homage to her. Dance
increases in tempo. WAZOBIA *joins them, takes over the*
dance from the hilarious crowd. Suddenly, she stops
dancing. The drumming ends abruptly, too, halting the
entire crowd. Momentary freeze. WAZOBIA *changes her*
countenance, fire of anger glittering in her eyes)
(to the women) Dance no more!

For ages, you have been dancing to
Feast the eyes of licentious men and
Visiting generals.
Dance no more!
What good has the gyration brought you?
Dance no more!
For ages they have used and sucked you
Dry and disposed of at will.
When will you learn?
Pause awhile. Ask yourselves
Why the law prescribes a female regent.
Where are the men
If rulership is the sole preserve of men?
Do you think they contradict themselves when
They make a female regent rule for only
Three seasons when a king passes beyond?
They plant us as king unasked
And supplant us at will.
I, Wazobia, know everything at my fingertips.
They, of their volition, threw the throne on
My lap, and lap it I must!
I remember it all,
How it all began, at least in my case.
If you have forgotten, I have not . . .
If you have forgotten, I, Wazobia, shall show you . . .
(Clapping of cymbals, drums mixed with xylophone are heard. Fade out on WAZOBIA *for flashback. Light changes to bluish green, filters to orange, until it spreads to red, filling the entire stage. The atmosphere is evidently charged. The clouds are laden with foreboding air of tension. The air is so thick you can cut it. It is the night of* WAZOBIA's *coronation as king-surrogate or regent to the throne of Ilaaa in Anioma kingdom. The late king, Ogiso, has just been laid to rest with his ancestors. The focus of attention is now the vacant throne and the tree stump significantly hedging it to mark the end of an era)*

PRIEST OF ANI: *(pouring a bottle of palm oil)*
Our fathers . . .
We your children have come to you.
You, whose eyes can see far behind and before us,
Send us rain

In these dark days of drought,
Spray us with your shower from the sky
To wipe away this salted rain
From our flabby faces in these days
Wearing the shroud of darkness. Send us light.
We do not command you,
We only ask that you show us
The way. You have the wisdom
To inquire, to ask questions,
For it was you who left us with the adage that
"A child who asks questions never misses the road."
We remember this wisdom and therefore have come to
    you.
(He throws pieces of kolanut on the Ikenga)
The great Iroko tree has fallen.
How long will the little birds be left
To wander and grope in the dark?
How long?
(He pours libation of palm wine on the earth)
You recalled your son, our great king, Ogiso,
To sit on your right hand,
Leaving our throne cold, dry, empty.
For this, we have come
To you, our father.
Show us from our midst
She who must bear this mantle,
Warming the seat of our heart, our land.
*(As he says the words, he places palm oil and a cockerel
on an ukpa and beckons* PRIEST OF OHENE *to carry it to its
destination)*
Your messenger to them at the bush path,
To them at the crossroads . . .
To them at the bottom of the sea . . .
*(*PRIEST OF OHENE *leaves with great expediency)*
Go, bear our burden to Ifejoku and Onokwu.
We long for rain that this stump may grow,
We long to plant new seed for fruit,
For harvest . . .
Tonight, the king-surrogate must be chosen.
Go, tell them that night oppresses us,
We long for rain . . .
We long for seed, for harvest . . .

(The PRIEST OF ANI *is suddenly interrupted by the* OMU, *Her Royal Highness, King of Women, leading the late king's wives like a herd of cattle. The king's wives are typically wrapped in mourning outfit: black piece of cloth, tied from chest down, no blouses, hair beadless, shaved right round and carved in bonds to number three. The* OMU *storms in, querying why she has been slighted in the rites)*

OMU: *(belligerently)*
Who talks about harvest in a season of drought?

PRIEST OF ANI:
I, the Priest of Ani, Omu!
It is a night of vigil.

OMU:
And will remain so!
How do you think
You can snap the finger without the
Right thumb?

PRIEST OF ANI:
I know the direction of your accusing finger.
Haa, women,
No matter how much you try to elevate them,
Never rise above petty squabbles

OMU:
And you call me woman?
I, the Omu, surpassed all women,
King among women?

PRIEST OF ANI:
King among women,
But woman all the same,
No matter how, I still smell woman in you.

OMU:
And is that why you must leave me out of
Such important rituals as Ifejoku?

PRIEST OF ANI:
Since when have women become the pillar of
The state?
Ifejoku is an affair of the land,
Bush clearing,
It concerns planting,
It concerns planning,

It concerns the affairs of the state.
Woman!
This is a night of vigil,
It's a time of silence, of peace . . .
What we men strive
To sew, to put together
That lobe which threatens ever
To split apart
Women like hens pecking for worms,
Always set apart the spheres.

OMU: *(furiously)*
Enough!
(She raises her hand to strike him, but he too, has his hand up, either in self-defense or for retaliation. Suddenly, cock crows, they all freeze momentarily. PRIEST OF ANI *breaking the silence)*

PRIEST OF ANI: *(resignedly)*
The gods of our land
Save us from the iron hands of women!
(Exit PRIEST OF ANI, *spraying nzu[5]), throwing pieces of kolanut on the earth to appease the gods as he recedes. Once he is gone,* OMU *kneels the women before her and begins to shave clean their hair as a mark of respect and honor for their departed husband. As this is being done, drum and xylophone sounds rise slowly until the priest storms the scene, jubilant, leading a group of dancing maidens in the arena.* OMU *remains, while women leave the arena as the* PRIEST OF OHENE *and dancing maidens arrive. The women, too, are happy because the shaving of their hair is the end of mourning. The* OHENE *priest carries a smoked pot of herbs on his head, a staff of office on the right, and osho[6] on the left hand. The* PRIEST OF OHENE, *like a juju priest, wears white skirt around his waist, and rattle beads jingle at the trim of the skirt. He also wears charms and amulets around his chest and upper arms. His entrance with the dancing*

[5]**Nzu:** White clay, chalklike substance used for rituals.
[6]**Osho:** A unique oblong-shaped, stuffed staff of office for priests serving the goddess of the sea, Onokwu. It is made up of cowries symbolic of the wealth of the sea. Onokwu is also the bringer of children and prosperity.

*maidens changes the entire character of the scene, and
the community ululates, for this happy entry signifies
that the Ifejoku rite (bush clearing) is over and that the
gods of the land are willing to accept their offering for
new planting, new seeds for growth. More important,
the success of this ritual is a positive development in
their quest to elect a female king-surrogate who will
rule for three seasons until a new male king is crowned.
The choice of the surrogate-king or regent will be made
from the dancing maidens who are daughters of the
land. The maidens dance for a while, finally forming a
cluster around the* OMU *and the* PRIEST OF OHENE *as the
chiefs arrive spread in a semicircle behind them. With
the entrance of the chiefs, the beat of the music changes
to more vibrant or masculine tune, and the priest begins to dance while the maidens, as if automated, stop
their own dancing. Then the* PRIEST OF ANI, *looking fero-
cious, arrives on the scene. He takes three long strides:
each time he throws nzu into the air as he mutters some
incantations. Once the* PRIEST OF ANI *takes over the scene,
bearing the crown on his left hand, and wielding a staff
of office in the air with the right hand, maidens stretch
their hands upward as if reaching into the sky and
freeze while the chiefs watch with anxious looks on
their faces. The king also can be seen at the periphery.
The drumming is still on, but once the priest throws his
staff upward, there is total hush until the staff lands on
the chosen one. It is* WAZOBIA. *All but* IYASE, IDEHEN, *and*
ANEHE *in the entire crowd take up the chorus "Wazobia!
Wazobia! Wazobia!" jubilating and ululating, dancing as
they do so. The dancing is so well choreographed that
their formation changes to a semicircle with* WAZOBIA
*standing in the middle and holding the staff downward.
Then* WAZOBIA, *smiling and in a very slow motion, begins
to raise the staff upward with her hand, the other on
her hip. Simultaneously, music wanes as the crowd
gradually stoops down. The* PRIEST OF ANI *steps forward,
adorns* WAZOBIA *with the king's regalia and crown. Final
beat of the drum, and at the same time, the* PRIEST OF
OHENE *lifts* WAZOBIA's *mother from the ground and sits
her down beside the throne. She is visibly elated. Everybody is down on his or her knees except* IYASE, *who is*

adamant and remains standing. Care should be taken to show the transition in WAZOBIA*'s personality here from a young maiden to an authoritative "king." The countenance on her face changes as she notices* IYASE*'s insubordination. Fear grips the crowd)*

WAZOBIA: *(authoritatively)*
You will kneel, Iyase!
(All eyes are now on IYASE*, fear written all over them,* IYASE *still adamant. Wazobia, vehemently)*
Kneel, Iyase!
*(*IYASE*, as if shaken by earthquake, begins to tremble, bending his knees until he finally succumbs, knees down, face down, hands tucked behind him. The drum gives one note of finality. The tight faces of the crowd spread into smiles and, kneeling straight, all stretch their hands skyward. Only* WAZOBIA *remains standing, smiling, looking triumphant among the kneeling crowd)*

CROWD:
Hail, Wazobia!
Hail our maiden king!
Hail, Wazobia!
Hail our new dawn!
Hail high our king!
Long reign Wazobia!
(Slow fadeout)

MOVEMENT TWO

Palace square. Crown sits on the throne. King's wives, in a state of flutter, darting from here to there in preparation for the king's entry. The women wear the typical woven white cloth tied above their chests, and their heads are adorned with beads. Whereas the younger wives weave their hair into three strands, the king's most senior wife, ANEHE *wears hers in one; the sides are shaven and the edge trimmed with a wand of beads. Each of them clutching her plate of food meant for the king seems to be vying for choice position around the*

possible path of entry of the king unto the throne. ANEHE
and WA *are the first to arrive.*

ANEHE:
Did you hear that they have taken Wazobia's mother
away?

WA:
But that is no news? It is the tradition. A king has neither
mother nor father. If any such parent lives, he or she must
go on some kind of exile. It's no news that a king's parents
must give way.

ANEHE:
What is news is that Kaanebi, a woman so wretched that
her husband pounded her like fufu and finally sent her
away will now be a queen-mother while we are still alive.
I will not be surprised if they build a palace for her.

WA:
Why all the fuss and pushing as if Wazobia is not a mere
girl, raised from the dust? *(Enter* BIA *and then* ZO*)*

BIA: *(interrupting)*
She may be a mere girl in your eyes, Anehe, but the gods
have anointed her.

ANEHE:
And is that why she now struts like a peacock?

ZO:
I would if I were her . . . Raised from the dregs of poverty
. . . Thanks to education! Wazobia, too, has every cause to
toast her power. Who would have thought that our regent
would come from a class of women whose eyes flame as
heat from the sun? Their feet so long they can stand on
the moon . . . *(Exit* ZO *and* BIA*)*

ANEHE:
And is that why Kaanebi, a nonentity, must
Shake her bottom like that as if I sit with my
Back? Does one show how much wealth one has
By oversalting the soup?
Strange, the way power transforms people.

WA:
And who do you blame?

ANEHE:

Indeed, who does one blame but the gods?
Sometimes I wonder if the gods are not blind after all.

WA:

It beats me, too, that the gods should bypass all the princesses in this royal house and choose a mere girl from
such an unclean home to rule us. *(Reenter* zo *and* bia
with their plates of food)

WA:

The gods sometimes act to humor us.

ZO: *(entering)*

It is the way of the gods . . .

WA: *(challenging)*

We are concerned with the way of the world.

BIA:

Speak not of the gods but of men.

ANEHE:

That is all you know!

BIA:

But we know that in the full glare of the world
Wazobia was crowned godhead.
The king is king, Anehe, whether you acknowledge it or
   not . . .
As humans bend for the door, so does the fowl . . .

ANEHE:

Ah, sharp tongue! Don't chop me off yet. I only made one
simple statement and there she splashes her mouthful of
spittle. Sell me! That is all the trade you know.

WA:

You, Anehe, should have known better not to make certain statements before a wireless radio.

ZO:

You women surprise me. I do not see anything
Wrong in what Bia said just now.

ANEHE and WA:

Why should you?

ANEHE:

After all, you all cringe and kneel, hoping to attract the
king's favor.

WA:

Must we beg the ground to walk on it? Must we cut our necks just because we do not belong? Just because they are hoping to be close to those who are close to power?

ANEHE:

Ever since Ogiso died, they won't let us hear in this house. And the water we drink must stick on our teeth just because the king is dead . . .

BIA: *(interrupting)*

Anehe, how can you talk like that?

ANEHE:

And why must I not talk like that? Is there a decree against talking?

BIA:

Yes, a decree.

ZO:

Against certain kinds of talk . . . Against reckless talk. Is it not abominable that a king's wife must be reminded that a king does not die?

ANEHE:

And what does he do if he doesn't die?

WA: *(sarcastically)*

He sails overseas . . .

ANEHE: *(chuckling)*

Hmm, there is nothing Anehe won't hear in this house where the air is full of their Wazobia. *(ANEHE and WA laugh mockingly)*

BIA:

But for Wazobia, you'll not be standing firm on the ground. You would have remained, tucked away, rejected today like pudding without wrap. A woman without husband is like pudding without wrap which feasts the eyes but which no one longs to have.

ANEHE:

We have heard, *ears* of the ruling house. The king does not die, and Wazobia has been crowned *Godhead* . . . *(As she says this, the sound of the drum/horn can be heard announcing the entrance of the king to the palace square. The lead drummer or horn blower renders the* traditional ituafa[7]; pouring encomiums on the king and tracing her pedigree. WAZOBIA inherits all the royal regalia of the late king, and from now on she can appear in public only in these royal outfits. On no occasion should she be dressed any longer as a woman. While the lead DRUMMER or horn blower chants the praise names, others respond in chorus. WAZOBIA sits on the throne acknowledging the praises)

DRUMMER:

Here comes the lion.

When the lion enters the arena,

Lesser animals search for their holes in earnest!

CHORUS:

So it is!

It is so!

DRUMMER:

The one who has the heart of a gun,

Descendant of warriors who drink with

Human heads,

Agadaga Agbogidi,

The one whose feet cause sudden tremors in the forest!

DRUMMER:

Child of Diji who eats yams with branches,

They who are masters of barns laden with yams,

Son of Diji, they who reap yams as huge as human bodies,

They who eat with both hands!

CHORUS:

So it is!

It is so!

DRUMMER:

Descendant of Omenka,

They who have such mastery

That they can put human form into the art of weaving,

I salute you!

CHORUS:

So it is!

It is so!

---

[7]**Ituafa:** Praise-singing, or oriki, whereby encomiums are chanted, highlighting the pedigree and unique qualities of the recipient.

DRUMMER:

I salute you, house of dry stick which remains standing when

Everyone expects it to fall.

And instead, the full-bodied tree bustling with life

Makes an undignified salute, greeting the sky

With its roots. I salute you!

CHORUS:

So it is!

It is so!

DRUMMER:

I salute you,

They who own trees

That bear money as fruits,

Agu!!8 I salute!

I salute you!

I salute you! Agu!

(The DRUMMER *or horn blower sounds the final note of greeting with the musical instrument. All the women who went down on their knees as soon as* WAZOBIA's *presence was announced begin to creep forward, vying for choice positions to attract the attention and favor of the king,* ANEHE *kneeling and thrusting her dish forward)*

ANEHE:

My king!

WA: *(kneeling and thrusting her dish forward, too)*

Eat, mine is sweetest!

ZO:

Eat, my king!

BIA:

Mine, my king . . .

*(*WAZOBIA *places her fly whisk/fan three times by way of salute or prayer on the head of each of the women. Brief pause)*

WAZOBIA:

Rise, rise, rise—my faithful ones.

Lest you sprain your knees.

It is no time to kneel but a time to stand.

8**Agu:** Lion.

(The women rise, and WAZOBIA *beckons them to sit down)*

It is no time to succumb but to stand, my women. It is no time to gloat on praises, women. The task ahead calls for abstinence and sacrifice. That we may not be too heavy to discharge . . .

(Enter OMU, *interrupting the conversation. She is quite agitated.* WAZOBIA *studies her. As soon as the* OMU *enters, the women who were hitherto relaxed begin to look panicky, falling down on their knees to greet her)*

OMU: *(tersely to* WAZOBIA*)*

Agu!

(No response. Brief silence)

WAZOBIA:

May I know what mission brings the Omu, first and mother of women with a tight face, to the royal throne of Anioma?

OMU:

And may I ask why the one who supposedly occupies the royal throne of Anioma will not take pains to know the angle the sun seats in the sky. Even a strange hen in a new house stands, one foot up, one foot down, surveying the territory with its ears and eyes . . .

Why, king,

Do these women

Sit here at the level of the throne while the chiefs and the entire kingdom await them to make their appearance at the marketplace so as to complete the funeral rites for the king that traveled. Why?

WAZOBIA:

Why, may I ask, must widows be subjected to the torment of incessant funeral rites that men are free of, under similar situations, Omu?

OMU:

It is our tradition that women who survive funeral rituals dance in the marketplace as final mark of their innocence regarding their husband's death. A woman who dies mourning is unclean and must be left to rot in the evil forest.

WAZOBIA: *(arrogantly)*

I see, Omu. My women will not dance naked in public to appease the eyes of a wrathful populace.

This is no era for dancing to entertain lustful eyes.

OMU: *(interrupting)*

But an era of what? This is no matter for big grammar or high-faluted "isms" and ideologies!

WAZOBIA:

But of what?

OMU:

Tradition. Tradition as we met it. Tradition passed down to us from the time when the world's eyes were still closed. Tradition handed down from generation to generation. Tradition . . . Tradition . . . Tradition . . . Wazobia . . .

WAZOBIA:

The face of the sun changes, so does the moon.
Seasons too change,
So does the face of the clock.
The clock ticks . . .

OMU: *(petulantly)*

I know not clock!
Clock know not me.
All I know is time
And my Oyibo.
Rain knows no king,
It falls when it must. There is a time for every purpose . . .
There is time for every purpose. . .
I am the Omu, the first and mother of all.
She who has cooked longer can boast of more broken
   pots . . .

WAZOBIA: *(smiling)*

We have heard. Longevity is no measure of wisdom. At least, not in our time. Sift from time what the time demands and promises. These women have more urgent roles than such ceremonies meant to extort the very last breath, wealth, and dignity from them! My women will not dance today!

OMU: *(scandalized)*

Ilaaa, come and see! Come and hear
What wind breaks from the mouth of a woman washed with the sand of this earth.[9]

---

[9]**Washed with the sand of this earth:** Any child born in Aniocha Igbo community (where this play is set) is first "washed" with the earth before any form of water and oil is put on his or her body.

Our Ilaaa . . .
It is early
That one must drive a black goat to roost in its pen.
Ilaa! Remove the hand of the monkey from the soup,
It looks too much like human hand . . .

WAZOBIA:

Do not dip your hand in uji agwo[10] lest the snake spit its
Venom on you.
You seek to keep the clock stand still, Omu,
But gravity must take its toll.
I will not be intimidated. For now, that is food enough.
Chew it.

OMU:

And I will not be party to the death of tradition.
The ones who hold the titles of the land must hear how
You misrule them.
(Exit OMU *in great anger.* WAZOBIA *rather calmly turns to
the women)*

WAZOBIA:

Women, that is the task before you,
To set the hand of the clock aright,
To move time, not allow time to move you . . .
It's our time to till. It's our time to tend,
That we may be planted on firm soil . . .
*(Suddenly, a woman runs into them screaming for
mercy, for protection. Following immediately behind
her is her assailant. The woman kneels before the king)*

WOMAN: *(gasping)*

My king!
I am in your hands!
Save me!

MAN: *(threateningly)*

You may run into a mouse hole.
These hands must teach you today that
They were not made of decaying plantain stem.
Come out and I'll show you . . .

WAZOBIA: *(to the man)*

Do you realize
That what you are doing now is against tradition?

---

[10]**Uji Agwo:** A grove around a tree containing dark water from the tree
or rainwater which villagers resort to at periods of drought. This kind
of grove is usually a fertile abode for snakes.

Tradition forbids you to touch anyone who has protection
Of another. And more so, your king?
Is it that men in these parts make traditions
For others to bear them?

MAN:

Tradition?
And is that why a woman,
A mere woman that I paid to get with my own hard-earned
money should challenge me in my house? Does she think
I carry these balls between my thighs for nothing?

WAZOBIA:

And this is an answer to your king?

MAN:

It is no matter for king and subject, but a matter for man
and woman. The gods of our land ordained that a man
must own a wife to bear him children . . .

WAZOBIA: *(interrupting)*

And did your gods also ordain that you must turn these
women to slaves?
That their tongues must be slashed for daring to see with
their eyes? And hear with their ears that dare to reveal to
them what tune time beats? You complain that their
hands are weak when you forbid them to use the hands.
You condemn their feet as frailty but shudder when they
want to stand firm on the soil . . .
This matter will not end here . . .
*(She strikes a bell by the side of the throne. The atten-
dant runs in in salutation)*

WAZOBIA:

Attendant, go immediately,
Tell the town crier to summon all the people.
(Exit attendant)
You may all leave me now.
(Exit all but WAZOBIA, *pensive. Once the gong of the* TOWN
CRIER *is heard, freeze on* WAZOBIA*)*

TOWN CRIER:

Kom! Kom! Kom! Ilaaa-aa.
The mouth of the king announces to you the king's
summons. Tomorrow, when the sun is overhead,
All . . . all sons and daughters of Anioma kingdom,
Old or young, must gather at the palace square.
This is the message!
I am only the bearer—ooooo!!!

Kom! Kom! Kom!
(Exit TOWN CRIER. WAZOBIA *treads gingerly as if counting her footsteps to the throne. She lowers herself to the royal seat. Slow fadeout)*

MOVEMENT THREE

(The palace square of Ilaaa. Time, noon. The entire kingdom is gathered, male and female, old and young. WA-ZOBIA, *in all her majesty, sits heavy on the throne. Behind her stands the attendant bearing the golden staff of office.* WAZOBIA *is visibly weighed down by the huge weight of office strung around her neck, arms, and ankles in the form of beads. The* DRUMMER *or the horn blower clears the air with his instrument, then the king begins her address)*

WAZOBIA:
Ilaaa Kwenu!

ALL: *(in chorus)*
Ei!

WAZOBIA: *(fast rhythm)*
Kwenu!

ALL: *(chorus reply fast, too)*
Eeii!!

WAZOBIA: *(faster rhythm)*
Kwenu!!

ALL: *(faster)*
Eei!!

WAZOBIA: *(faster still)*
Kwe zue nu!!!

ALL: *(faster still)*
Eei!!!

WAZOBIA:
My dear sons and daughters of the soil!
They whose umbilical cords were buried right at the root

of trees in this very soil [11]

It is I, your king, who speaks. I speak to you, not with the limited tongue of my fathers, but with many tongues acquired from sojourns here and beyond the seas. Our people, your king has called you to share our thoughts on the rules of governance. It is a new planting season.

We must till and toil together for growth.

IYASE: *(standing)*

Then, king, if we must deliberate on such serious state matters, women and the youth must be sent away!

(IYASE sits. The men nod their approval)

WAZOBIA:

I do not see any reason why women and youths must be kept away from matters of state concern. Matters of state affect them much as they affect chiefs and princes.

(The chief and men murmur their discontent; some even whisper to their neighbors)

IYASE: *(standing)*

I support what my fellow chief, Iyase, has to say. Serious matters of state concern are too heavy for the brittle heads of women and children.

(It is now obvious that the women are getting quite uneasy)

OZOMA: *(cautiously)*

Ehn, ehm, I have looked at the coin from both sides. My fellow chiefs, although we know what tradition demands and commands, I suggest that we allow the throne to exercise some executive prerogative. We know our youths travel far and wide nowadays. Let them lend us the benefit of their sojourn beyond our land . . .

IYASE: *(amused)*

What benefit, Ozoma?

What benefit have youths when they come home to dance or walk on their heads and wriggle their bodies like boas about to pounce on their victims? Or like people suffering from epileptic fits, and they call it break dancing? What

---

[11]**Umbilical cord buried at the root of the tree:** When a child is born in Aniocha Igbo community, the dry umbilical cord which usually falls off after the first week of birth is buried at the root of a fruit tree which could then be regarded as the child's roots and tree of life.

benefit is that to our land, Ozoma? You who see the oath
but prefer to swear by the fire? What benefit, Ozoma?

IDEHEN:

That of the youth is even better. Can you imagine
What foul air oozes from the mouths of our wives
spreading
Such slogans as *women liberation?*
Women *emancipation!*

IYASE: *(still amused)*

Liberation from what? From the kitchen or from where?

IDEHEN:

Emancipation from lying below to lying on top!
*(The men laugh. The women have become so uneasy
that they begin to stand up to leave.* WAZOBIA, *who has
been watching calmly, now changes her countenance)*

WAZOBIA: *(authoritatively)*

Women, I order you to stay!

IYASE:

And men insist that women must leave this gathering!
(This is followed by a chorus of voices of the men)

OMU:

That is what happens when you bring long-legged and
senseless goats from up north who do not understand
your ways to rule you.

WAZOBIA: *(striking the royal bell beside her)*

Now, *silence!* The king decrees!

IYASE: *(aside to* IDEHEN)

Our fathers ruled us by debate.
They rule us by decree!

WAZOBIA:

I know when men are united. When they have a common
enemy. That is *woman.* The king will not allow himself to
be dragged into the mud of your prejudices. *He,* the king,
She is beyond man or woman. The king has therefore
gathered you, to make this pronouncement. That whatever you call yourself, You are, every one of you, first and
foremost, *human beings* with potentials waiting to be ac-
tualized for the benefit of this kingdom!

IYASE: *(sarcastically)*

Perhaps this morning, our king has taken a shot of gin too
many. It may be necessary for him . . .

IDEHEN:

For *her*!

IYASE: *(chuckling)*

It is only women who see stars with a few cups of gin.

OZOMA:

Why don't you let the king speak?

IYASE: *(spitefully)*

Ozoma, sit down!

People must count their teeth with their tongues before they speak. Certain creatures must not open their mouths when *men* who are *men* stand up to speak!

(OZOMA, insulted and charged, gives a glare at IYASE. Brief silence)

IDEHEN:

When people talk about bones rattling, the old woman must sit back and wince, Ozoma.

To give token titles to strangers does not mean we have lost count of the trees that are homegrown. Ilaaa knows where the umbilical cords of its true sons are buried, deep in the roots of our soil. That the he-goat wears a beard does not mean that men must now say to it, "Good-morning sir."

(OZOMA, peeved, is poised to attack IDEHEN, who is also battle ready, but WAZOBIA strikes the royal bell. Women linger on. Freeze and then silence)

WAZOBIA:

Hold it! And sit down!

(Women obey, WAZOBIA rises, hush in the crowd)

Daughters and sons of Ilaaa! For centuries men have ruled . . .

For centuries men have ruled . . . misruled us . . .

The vandalism you saw a moment ago is only a minor testimony of their era of misrule.

Time, blind like rain, knows no king.

Time has come for you to hear some home truths. That we have kept quiet and observed your excesses . . . your excesses these long seasons do not mean we lack the words. Nor do we lack the power to curb male excesses. Time has come for us to point the new directions of our rulership. We must begin with the man who pursued his wife, straight into the palace. Where is the woman abused? Stand, woman! Let the world see how your body has been turned into an accident car for panel beating.

(People, especially women and children, look around with questions written on their faces in search of the victim and the culprit. The WOMAN *stands. All eyes are now on her husband, who remains seated. But while the women look excitedly with victory written on their faces, the men remain generally calm, unperturbed)*

Will that brute stand? Stand before this gathering for all to see!

(The MAN, *adamant, does not stand, but the eyes of the crowd have already identified him. Brief silence. Wazobia, pointing)*

You are the man.

Why do you remain seated

When the king commands?

MAN:

You called for the brute. I am no brute.

WAZOBIA:

Then what are you? What name do you on Earth call yourself

When you pound a grown woman like fufu in a mortar?

(The men are now becoming irritable)

MAN:

I thought women boast of power; of being equal in every-thing to men.

If the fowl boasts that urinating is an easy matter, let it urinate for the world to see.

IYASE: *(standing to support him)*

This looks like an inquest. It is not the way things are done traditionally. Let the man state his case. If he is guilty, then you can pass your sentence on him.

MAN:

I have said it time and time again,

I will offer myself for castration

The day I allow a woman

That I paid for with my own money

To lie on my top and taunt me with her fingers.

Tell me how,

In my own house,

Why I should come home

And not find my food
With my woman waiting on the table.

WOMAN:

Why not? Of course, I am part of the furniture in your
   house
And once you come home
You have a ready platform to sit on.
You pursue lizards while those with whom you started
Now pursue rats.
And I must go in search of the food
You must eat.
Must I not leave the house to fetch that food?

MAN:

What does she expect when I come home and not find her
With my food on the table?
My people,
Does one have breasts and suck from the hump of a tree?

WOMAN:

Why won't you come home every day from your concu-
   bine to
Find me fixed,
Attending your food on the table?

WAZOBIA:

And is that her offense?

IYASE:

Women, no matter what status they claim to have, women
are highly provocative.

WAZOBIA: *(vehemently)*

Nobody has asked you to speak, Iyase!

IYASE: *(stuttering)*

But . . . , but. . . .

WAZOBIA:

I have the floor! Sit down!
(IYASE *obeys. Total silence, but the air is now full of
tension)*
Now hear our manifesto. Henceforth the symbol of our
kingdom shall be the palm tree which from top to bottom
has all and produces all: from leaves, to thatch, to shade,
to brown.
From fruit, to wine, to oil, to kernel . . .

That is the palm. Each part, its own value and yet interdependent on all other parts. We all, man, woman, child, must be schooled. To actualize these potentials for full benefit, for all with none posing an obstacle to another, with the left hand washing the right, and the right hand the left. Henceforth women will have equal representation in rulership.

(The men grumble and boo to register their disapproval. Women shout, "Long reign Wazobia")

Schools will be built

To tutor women and bring out the best of their potentials,

To sharpen their awareness . . .

(The men are becoming more irritated) Henceforth, women shall have equal rights of inheritance in matters of land and property! Today we put a final seal on wife battering. A decree is hereby promulgated on wife beating.

For none is slave to another. Man and woman decreed as partners in progress, not antagonists. This is why the man who beat his wife must tender his apology now before all. *(At this point, the man who was humiliated for beating his wife takes a stride or two in front of his wife)*

MAN: *(assertively)*

I have not done anything that is abominable in the custom of our land. As our fathers did, so must we. A set tradition does not kill a bride. We cannot sew a bag for long things and then kill a snake and carry it with our bare hands. If this is the future we build for our world, I wish not to belong to it!

(Suddenly, he raises his cloth from behind, baring his bottom for his wife to see before all. This singular act is called Ikpoike, and it is the traditional method of declaring that a man has divorced his wife. The result is that it has caused a general stir and excitement in the crowd. Once the MAN has completed that act, he stages a walkout. Other men, particularly chiefs, follow suit in support of the MAN. The OMU follows, too. The women break into a dance in celebration of their freedom. They end the dance with a shout of "Long Reign Wa-zo-biaaa!")

BIA:

We have taken over the stage.

Women have taken over the stage.

ZO:

Except the Omu.

WAZOBIA:

Don't mind her. She suffers from intellectual menopause.
Someone go and invite the Omu to our royal presence.

*(A woman leaves immediately. She soon returns with
the* OMU, *who with disgust stares from* WAZOBIA *to the
other women)*

OMU: *(to* WAZOBIA*)*

Tell me what you have invited me for. Or have you called
me again to tell me how backward I am?

To show where my Chi[12] has branded me with a scar?

Wazobia,

Wazobia, take heed.

You cannot change the course of things. Never can water flow

From the foot to the head.

Wa-zo-bia,

Wazobia of hard hearing,

When a breast has fallen, it has fallen,

Never again to stand erect, Wazobia . . .

WAZOBIA: *(calmly)*

Omu! Queen and mother of the tribe! First among
women. Thumb without which other fingers cannot snap.
Look around you. There are no strange faces here! Only
your children surround you. For long, men have had their
baths with the tears of your daughters, Mother. For long,
their eyes have been covered to shield them from seeing,
from knowing the truth. Look around you, Omu! Women
have ears. Why must they be prevented from hearing with
them? Women have heads. Why must they be stuffed with
cotton wool only useful for cleaning up their men?
Women have hands. Why must they not be allowed to use
them fully to construct? Who among you here can weave?
(Some raise their hands) Go take up your looms and
weave. Who among you here can trade? *(Others raise
their hands)* Go weave to cover us from our nakedness.
And so on and so on. With or without man, make a meaning of your life.

(Slowly, the OMU *is beginning to relax her stern face, and*

---

[12]**Chi:** God of fortune.

gradually she becomes so persuaded that by the time WAZOBIA *makes the last statement, the* OMU's *face has thawed out completely into a smile, and she spreads her hands, encompassing all the women who have risen in unison to form a circle around her. All the women break into a triumphant song. Blackout)*

MOVEMENT FOUR

IDEHEN'S *house. It is twilight.* IDEHEN *paces up and down. It is obvious that he is disturbed. He sits down in an easy chair, tries to puff at his pipe, but even this distraction would not suffice. He takes up his red cap for chiefs, holds it up, staring at it for a while with rapt interest. He soon begins to lose interest in this regard, and as if all the venom in him is now rushing to his fingers, he flings the cap to the door which has remained shut.*

IDEHEN:
What use am I? A toy cap in the fingers of a mere woman. What use am I? A chief they call me who can stand on two feet and ten toes and allow a woman, a mere woman, to clear her rotten throat and spit the phlegm at my face? As night overtakes day, we sit in complacency, while Wazobia . . . Wazobia wears the crown and stands between us. Wazobia. That log lodged on us. Wa-zo-bia. That log lodged between ambition and the throne playing on these balls with ease. *(Pause, and, as if recollecting something, he begins to smile)* But . . . but Wazobia is a woman. A woman is a woman. Whether she lies high or low. I too must push my balls into net, I know I can . . . But . . . but I must first play out Iyase. Iyase is second in rank in the hierarchy of the throne of Ilaaa. I, Idehen, the cat whose back never touches the ground on a wrestling arena, a mere runner-up. Iyase is my bait. That friendly fox preying around the chicks who with a mere grain and cackle, rush in. But Iyase is past master at this game. But I, Idehen, surpass all craft and graft. With the women behind Wa-

zobia, and with Wazobia tucked between my thighs, Iyase will be sold off. To sell is not to be sold. Tonight, I prepare my broth for Wazobia. With Iyase as the condiment. Iyase is my friend, but that, too, does not mean that the fowl should feed into the stomach of the goat . . .

(IDEHEN *becomes more excited and even breaks into a dance step. A knock at the door.* IDEHEN *is too engrossed in savoring his dreams when* IYASE *enters the room, and* IDEHEN, *unaware of his presence, trips on him with both of them nearly tumbling to the ground. Only the wall wedges them.* IDEHEN *is definitely embarrassed, stupefied. He opens his lips to say something, stutters, and shuts them again)*

IYASE: *(attempting to regain his balance)*
Odia ekele ogede eme ka ji . . .

IDEHEN: *(recovering from shock but still staggering)*
Em . . . em . . . em . . .

IYASE:

Get the pieces of yourself together, man. Or has Wazobia so shattered you that she has crushed the balls between your thighs?
Has Wazobia empowered herself with your manhood?

IDEHEN: *(steadying himself)*
Times are treacherous, Iyase.
The sun sets in on us. And the day is no longer as it was when morning began.

IYASE:

I know what you mean, Idehen.
Times are hard,
But if darkness does not come,
One cannot criticize the day

IDEHEN:

I am trying,
We are trying,
Even when darkness gives way,
Betraying our dreams to light.

IYASE:

It is not time to lament
But a time to plot our future.
Bedbug once told her children
That whatever is hot will go cold.

IDEHEN:
Yes, Iyase,
But one must never underrate one's enemy.
The beginning of victory is a true assessment and under-
    standing
Of the strength of the enemy.
Wazobia is hot soup
That must be eaten
Not from the center
But slowly from the sides.
For us to succeed, Wazobia must fall from the heights
To which she has risen,
Spraying her piss in our mouths,
Wazobia must fall.

IYASE:
That we may rise.

IDEHEN: *(apprehensively)*
Did you say "that *we* may rise"?

IYASE: *(he, too, becoming suspicious)*
Ehm, eh . . . No . . . No, not really. Eh, what I have come
for, actually, is for us to put heads together on how to
dislodge Wazobia from the throne.

IDEHEN: *(aside)*
That you may sit squarely on the throne?

IYASE:
How can we, grown men, be begging the Earth
To set foot on our own soil?

IDEHEN:
It is abominable.

IYASE:
And worse still, that such injury should be inflicted on us
by a chaff of grain. Wazobia, whose father, a pauper, could
not beat his chest before men who were men?

IDEHEN:
We are failures to our ancestors. Were we not here when
the white missionaries came in to us and began to inocu-
late the so-called Christianity with its extended family of
education and equality? Now the toxic effect takes hold
of our ranks. The osu, the social outcasts, and the poor
were the first to drink from the contagious water of the
white men. The outcasts were the first to be curdled in the

embrace of the Whitebody.[13] Now we are all locked in the leprous grip of the disease of freedom.

IYASE:

We cannot blame ourselves, but the gods.

At times, I wonder if the gods have gone blind.

IDEHEN:

You cannot blame the gods, either. Sometimes the gods like to humor us in our shame.

IYASE:

Yes, I agree with you. Rather than chase them away, we welcome them in our midst, all because of the promise of coins. Money! Money! That opium that sent us to sleep while the strangers slept with our women, leaving us with the Wazobias. They embalmed us with money, and we began to court these people who had the advantage of white wealth. The white disease!

We must catch the lion by getting hold of its cub. In spite of the avowed solidarity, women are women. You cannot rule out petty jealousies among them.

Throw a grain of maize on a brood of chicks. Grip the hen as they cackle for the booty . . .

(At this point, BIA has entered the premises, but she is not seen by the chiefs, who are lost in their thought. She hides by the wall, eavesdropping on them)

I personally, shall use Wazobia's women against her.

IDEHEN:

Who precisely?

IYASE:

Anehe and Wa. I know they do not like Wazobia.

IDEHEN: *(thoughtfully)*

I see. Well, we shall see how the python basks in the sun . . .

IYASE:

But that is only one strategy. Wazobia has stayed beyond her limit.

She is only a regent.

And tradition stipulates

That a regent can reign for only three seasons.

The chiefs know this,

---

[13]**Whitebody:** Igbo euphemism for leprosy.

The men know this,
It is a very easy argument, persuading them to force
Wazobia down from the throne.
Men will depose Wazobia.
Wazobia, that fattened cow, must crumble.
Tomorrow, we assemble
All the chiefs and men of Ilaaa.
The black goat must be chased in to roost early, lest it
    stray into night,
Damaging valuable barns.

IDEHEN:

Tomorrow, then . . .

IYASE:

At the palace square . . .
*(The night is fading. Dim light, filtering through the xy-
lophone or drum sounds as the transition from night to
day, gradually reveals the palace grounds)*

MOVEMENT FIVE

Still dark, IDEHEN *creeps into the palace. Sitting on the
throne is* WAZOBIA's *crown.* IDEHEN *looks at the crown
longingly, takes a pace or two toward it, retreats, re-
peats the same motion, stretching his arms to take up
the crown and place it on his own head. He is trying the
crown on his head, adjusts it with his hands and neck
to fit into his head, when suddenly someone coughs.*
IDEHEN, *stultified, embarrassed, and nearly choking
from the shock of being apprehended, falls belly down
in absolute prostration to the one who has just
emerged. It was* WAZOBIA. IDEHEN, *fretting, greets. With
each greeting, he stands, prostrates, hitting his fore-
head on the ground in absolute submission.*

IDEHEN:

Agu! Agu! Agu!
*(*WAZOBIA *observes him coldly but studiously as he re-
sponds to the greetings, raises her fan to the sky with*

each response. Pause. IDEHEN, *rising, holding his own cap on his hand and smiling sheepishly)*

IDEHEN:

Hm . . . em . . . em . . .

WAZOBIA: *(snobbishly)*

May I ask what mission brings the lion in a lamb shed covered by the face of the dark?

IDEHEN:

Agu!

*(*IDEHEN *draws a step or two near* WAZOBIA *when she halts him with a motion from her hand.* IDEHEN *halts, scratches his head as if to recover confidence that has taken flight from there.* WAZOBIA *is now seated)*

IDEHEN: *(more assuredly)*

As a matter of fact, king, I have come, not as a lion, to scare the lambs, but as a friend and shepherd of the lamb. I must begin by first making my apology for seem-ing to be in agreement with your enemies against you. But I have been doing it for a purpose: love.

WAZOBIA: *(curious)*

Love?

IDEHEN:

Yes, love for you!
My throne . . . my king!
Ugbana, the bird of unalloyed whiteness!
Ozugwe, the king and beauty of snakes!
Ekenogwulugwu, Agu!
Rainbow whose many colors dazzle the sky!
Rainbow which commands the sky,
Taunting the Earth with her tears and smiles!
Rainbow whose laughter
Shakes the land, leaving the water loaded!
Master of the sky!
Mistress of the land whose voice thunders through trees,
Breaking dissident branches,
Bending willing branches.
Agu . . . I salute you . . . I salute you.

WAZOBIA: *(interrupting)*

Enough of that now! Enough!
What brings you to the palace?

IDEHEN:

Your safety, my king.

WAZOBIA: *(laughing sarcastically)*
A moment ago, it was love, now it is my safety.
Chief though you are, I have every right to demand that you be locked up. The finger that exceeds the navel must explain its mission!

IDEHEN:
My king,
Your life is in danger.
Iyase, your second in command, trails you dangerously.
(This information makes WAZOBIA *start, almost jumping from her seat)*
Iyase's eyes stare colored on the throne.
Do not say I told you. But, my king,
Because I love you, because I care for your safety,
I have joined to sap their secrets for our good. The greatest weapon of one who fights is to know not just the weakness of his enemies but their secret and strength, too. I have discovered that Iyase has plans to unseat you for his own elevation.

WAZOBIA: *(warming up more toward* IDEHEN*)*
Yes, go on; unfold the sleeves of thoughts tucked under populist garb to veil the men who put red on the face of truth to blind the eyes of the unconscious mind.

IDEHEN: *(excitedly)*
Iyase plans to crush you. Using us all as paste to gum himself on the throne. I have known this all along. I have trailed them all along to buffer myself up with more of their secrets. To share with you, to lay plans that will set you at right angles on the throne, this is the package of my love. Now that you have allowed me to unfold it, keep our secret secret. All I ask is to be allowed to share, to have now what you hold and after.

WAZOBIA: *(thoughtfully)*
Idehen, I am indeed grateful that you have me uppermost in your thoughts. I am willing to open up to you and share with you . . .
(They hear somebody cough, followed by footsteps. IDEHEN *is already beating a retreat when* BIA *enters)*

WAZOBIA: *(a bit embarrassed)*
Well, well, my faithful one, what keeps you awake at this time of the night?

BIA:

You, my king and master.

WAZOBIA:

Go in, it is not dawn yet.

I know you will always worry about me. Go in and sleep.

I know I am in safe hands.

BIA:

That is where you give me cause for concern, my king.

When you lie safe in their hands

To finger and poke nails into you until they crush you, my
  king . . .

Idehen is a man you must fear.

WAZOBIA:

Ah?

Idehen, too?

BIA: *(laughing)*

Ahn.

It is all planned, Idehen is Iyase, Iyase is Idehen. They see
you with blood flowing to their thumbs and nails. They
have plans, or rather each of them nurtures his own plans.
Both combined will unseat you, my king. Be careful, my
master and mistress.

WAZOBIA:

Idehen? Iyase? Planning to betray me? But these are my
chiefs! We should hold the cabinet together for our people whose future we hold in our hands. But why would
Idehen come to me if he holds this against me?

BIA:

In the final analysis, every man fights his own battle, only
teaming up with others when there is a common enemy.
This is the secret of their mission. Men tread and tend
crooked paths.

WAZOBIA:

But they are my chiefs!

Who among them can I now trust?

BIA:

Ozoma seems to be the most straightforward among
them. But even then, he is powerless because he is a
stranger who came and established himself and was hon-
ored with the chieftaincy title. This is why you cannot rely
on his strength to conquer them. They, too, know it.

WAZOBIA: *(upset)*

I am sick, sick and tired of plots by these ungovernable people. How much more should I sacrifice my time and life to set aright the lost foot of this generation

Only to get scalded in the process?

Perhaps, it is no use

Trying . . . trying . . . any . . . anymore . . .

(WAZOBIA's composure begins to falter. She fights hard to hold back her tears, when ZO runs in excitedly. WAZOBIA, bracing up, returns to her inner chamber, leaving BIA and ZO in front of the throne)

BIA: *(to ZO)*

You seem so excited. What is the matter?

ZO:

Tell me first, what is wrong

With our king and husband?

BIA:

Nothing serious. She is just tired.

ZO:

Of what?

BIA:

Well, leave that for now. Tell me what brought you that your eye flashes such light in the dark. One can see with them . . . these your little eyes like stars in an early morning.

(ZO holds BIA conspiringly, leading her in the direction of the village, when suddenly IYASE and ANEHE begin to emerge. ZO and BIA retreat and hide behind the throne to eavesdrop on IYASE and ANEHE)

IYASE:

Be careful. You know your fellow women can easily betray you.

ANEHE:

No, Wa is different. We both share together. With her and this plant as enzyme, our plans will speed up.

IYASE:

Wazobia may fall sooner than we expect. This day, before sunrise, the chiefs and men of Ilaaa will gather at the square. We must argue for her deposition . . .

ANEHE:

And if she refuses?

IYASE:

A simple matter. The people's will *will* prevail. The people will present Wazobia with steaming herbs in a pot when the people make such demands. It is a vote of no confidence on the king. It is a subtle piece of advice for such a king to disappear into the evil forest. He will either proceed on self-exile or commit suicide. Either way, Wazobia will receive a hot gift from the people.

ANEHE:

That is if you all reach that consensus.
And with such a woman-wrapper like Ozoma always on
   the side of the king
To bask in kingly favors, the task is as huge as lifting the
Earth herself.

IYASE:

Well, we shall see.

ANEHE:

Go now,
It is nearly cock-crow,
Lest the sun rise before us.

IYASE: *(departing)*

May our wish guide us.

IYASE: *(to* ANEHE*)*

Whose turn is it
To cook for your king today?

ANEHE:

Well, that is another problem. Since Wazobia ascended the throne, most traditions have been turned upside down. Wives no longer take turns to cook and compete for their husband's tongue and stomach. Wazobia insists that we all cook and share together. Reducing us all to the same level. There is no longer any incentive to try.

IYASE:

Don't let that bother you, my sweet one.
Kings reign only for a season. Wazobia's reign is even for a shorter season. Let her sow that we may reap. Pray that I get there.
*(*IYASE *points at the throne. He walks to the throne, sits right there with* ANEHE *on his lap. He bears a passionate look in his eyes)*

IYASE:

Anehe, the throne is only a foot away from me as second in command. I know I will get there. With you, I will get there. That is why you must help to speed up Wazobia's exit.

(IYASE tucks his hand into the cloth wrapped around his waist. He brings out a plant which he gives to ANEHE)

IYASE:

If only you can cook this potion,
Wazobia will be no more

ANEHE: *(accepting the plant)*

But Wazobia and I never get along well.
She knows that I resent her.

IYASE:

Try, by all means.

ANEHE:

I know what I will do. I will go through Wa.

(Exit IYASE. ANEHE stands awhile, studying the plant in her hand. Her lips part into a smile as she nods her head and runs into the inner chamber of the palace. As soon as she is gone, BIA and ZO emerge from hiding, regarding each other with shock written on their faces)

ZO: *(agitatedly)*

You have heard and seen with your eyes.
What do we do now?

BIA:

We must not tell the king. *She . . . he* is upset already.

ZO:

I know. I could sense that when I first entered.
Do you think he knows already?

BIA:

The king is gifted with a lot of insight.
I cannot tell precisely. But things are taking a dangerous turn.

ZO:

I know what we can do. Go brief Omu. Fetch her and other women here to the palace square while I go lock in Anehe and Wa that the plan of their plant may not take root. Time is of the essence. The cock will crow any time from now. We all meet here. Now is the time before sunrise. *Go!*

(Light fades. Exit BIA and ZO with slow mournful tune of

the flute following their steps. zo *returns shortly.* BIA
and OMU *soon join, immediately followed by other
women. The air feels very tense)*

OMU: *(clearing her throat)*

Daughters and women of Ilaaa!

CHORUS OF WOMEN:

Eei!

OMU:

When the house is on fire, it is no time for long greetings.
A man does not go chasing rats in the bush when his
house is on fire. Until our great king opened my eyes, I
was not aware what heat women steamed in,
But *now,*
Thanks to our great king who pulled the veil from *my*
and *your* eyes that we may further the cause of women.
The palace is under threat. Men are poised to throw
Wazobia into the seas as sacrifice.
To appease their ego, dethroned; for daring to smear
  their ego; for daring to tell
you women that you have the right to exist,
That you have hands,
That you have heads,
That you have eyes,
That you have ears,
That you have feet,
Which men insist that you use only occasionally, only for
their own purpose.

CHORUS OF WOMEN:

And we say *no!*

OMU:

This is why you must stand behind Wazobia with your bo-
som, your bosom, your king, that men will not penetrate.
At this very moment, men hold their meeting to unseat
Wazobia.
Wazobia is us.
We are Wazobia.
Together we stand. What they plan is abominable, and we
shall match force with force.
Together, join hands.
(The women obey)
Together we form this moon shape. Lie in ambush sur-
rounding the throne as the men emerge. We, together in

this naked legion, will salute them in our natural state. Taunting their eyes with their own shame. This naked dance is a last resort women have had over the ages. If our men force us to the wall, we must use it as our final weapon. Unusual problems demand unusual solutions.

(While the women still hold hands, zo runs to invite the king and returns shortly. wazobia walks into the palace, perplexed at what she sees before her. omu disengages herself from the arc the women have formed to enable her to explain things to wazobia who is now in the front center of the arc)

OMU:

Our great king,

We, your people, have come together to form this arc around you. That you may continue to reign for our own glory. That the world may see. We form this arc. To shield us from the stampede of masquerades.

WAZOBIA:

Masquerades? But there is no death in the clan? Masquerades, shadows of our ancestors, only visit when there is a new entrance to their world.

OMU:

Our great king. This is no time to ask questions. Night is around us. Pray for dawn. That masquerades may not evoke eternal darkness on us. Our king, you may leave us. *(Exit wazobia)* Women, remember your position *around* the throne. Stay in position. Stay in wait.

At cock-crow, take your position. So be it.

(The women retreat behind the throne. wazobia reenters with a frightful look in her eyes. She is alone, gazing and pacing from one end of the throne to another. The women lurk behind the throne. wazobia does not notice them at all)

WAZOBIA:

Masquerade?

Masquerade?

Masquerade?

Why masquerade?

(She is still lost in thought when light fades on her into the next scene)

MOVEMENT SIX

Drum sounds can be heard from a distance. The men and chiefs of Ilaaa have gathered in the palace square. Thick silence. Seated in front of the gathering is a calabash with rope hanging around its neck and a clay pot with herbs steaming. IYASE *takes the floor.*

IYASE:
Ilaaa Kwenu!

CHORUS OF MEN:
Eei!

IYASE:
Kwenu!

CHORUS OF MEN:
Eei.

IYASE:
Kwenu!

CHORUS OF MEN:
Eei.

IYASE:
Kwezue nu.

CHORUS OF MEN:
Eeee.

IYASE: *(chewing his words)*
Sons and chiefs of Ilaaa, We all know why we have gathered here. It is unusual for us to meet at this hour of the night, but as our ancestors say, all is not well when you see the frog hopping in the daylight. We have all been witness to the excesses of the one called king. The Wa-zo-bia, the new disease that plagues us.
Wa-zo-bia
The new wine that intoxicates, sending our women to run amok on the streets, throwing their dignity behind. No matter what happens, women are women. Like children, an overdose of this new wine, baptized as freedom by Wazobia, is bound to turn them giddy. That we may keep our balance, this new tail or wing by women must be clipped. Lest they take to flight and soar above us, their head. Water can never flow from the foot to the head.

We are the head, women can never rule us.
Sons of Ilaaa,
Do I speak your mind?

CHORUS OF MEN:

Of course you do!

IYASE:

Therefore, let us all purge ourselves of what aches us within. Speak! Men of Ilaaa!

(IYASE *takes his seat.* IDEHEN *rises to speak*)

IDEHEN:

Sons of Ilaaa, a strange thing is happening in our land. While we watch with our naked eyes, and with our hand clasped between our thighs, the hawk takes flight with our chicks. If we do not lick our lips, the harmattan takes over and licks them for us. *How?* With what mouth will it be said that we sons of Ilaaa lost our manhood with a sweep of a woman's hand? That what we men strive to put together women in their natural state set apart with their thighs setting the world ablaze in naked flame? How long must we succumb?

Know it, sons of Ilaaa, no matter what women do, a breast which has fallen has fallen. Nothing you can do again to make it stand erect.

Sons of Ilaaa,
Take what belongs to you by right. We know women,
They are not doing this all by themselves.

You must know that when a child dances by the footpath, its drummer must be playing in a nearby bush. Some of us here for want of favor are guilty of fueling the cause of women.

OZOMA: *(standing)*

Idehen, well you have spoken. We know where the finger points. But before we do that, we must first be sure of ourselves. He who says the fowl developed teeth overnight must first say who planted them.

IYASE: *(interrupting* OZOMA*)*

No! No! Ozoma. Leave that alone. We do not have time to pick petty quarrels here in the dark. But to put heads together for a lasting solution to this problem that plagues our ranks. We are there to expose . . . to dislodge . . . Wazobia's excesses.

IDEHEN: *(correcting)*
To purge her of those excesses.

IYASE:
Well, purging may not be lasting enough. It is a woman's nature to feed on excess. Soon the stomach is again empowered to bloat.

IDEHEN:
Wazobia is like a decaying tooth which must be extracted from the mouth of this clan.

CHORUS OF MEN: *(rising in anger)*
Extract the decaying tooth!
Oust Wazobia! Extract Wazobia!
Oust Wazobia!
(IYASE, satisfied that this potion is beginning to take effect)

IYASE:
Yes, extract Wazobia, but remember Wazobia is hot soup
Which must be eaten slowly . . .

IDEHEN:
And from the sides, too!

CHORUS OF MEN:
We want Wazobia out!
Oust Wazobia!
Out Wazobia!
Oust Wazobia!
Oust Wazobia!
(The mob rises in anger)

IYASE: *(halting them)*
Caution!
Wazobia is still king.
A king is not thrown into the soup pot like a fowl.

IDEHEN:
There are due processes for the deposition of a king.
Tradition, constitution provides for it. Fetch the high
    priest;
Present the hot calabash.

IYASE:
The pot steaming with heat.

IDEHEN:
With that heat on her hand, the fate that awaits all
    autocrats,

Wazobia will walk backward into the evil forest.
Wazobia will walk backward to be seen no more.

CHORUS OF MEN: *(now like a mob)*
Present her with the hot calabash.
The calabash!
The calabash!
Hot pot for Wazobia.
Hot pot for Wazobia.
Oust Wazobia!
Out Wazobia!

IYASE: *(calmly)*
You want your king deposed, then?

CHORUS OF MEN:
Yes!

IDEHEN:
Sons of Ilaaa! It is your choice! May your will be done!
(OZOMA rises, stares scornfully from IYASE to IDEHEN and back again, and then stages a dignified walkout. The other men coo and boo at OZOMA)

CHORUS OF MEN:
Shame! Shame!
Out Wazobia's wrapping cloth. Out woman wrapper!
Out those who have sold their manhood!

IYASE:
Someone go fetch the priest. The priest of Ani.
(The men continue their row until the priest arrive, the PRIEST OF ANI blowing his flute or horn. Calm returns to the gathering)

IYASE: *(to the priests)*
We sons and holders of the titles of this land, we have gathered together. The sons of Ilaaa demand that you who uphold our shrines, the abode of our fathers, that you who intercede between us and our father must carry the heat of our anger to Wazobia. We demand that you present the hot calabash to Wazobia, the butterfly king.
(The priests look at each other)

PRIEST OF ANI: *(perplexed)*
We, my fellow priest, and I, would like to go out and chew your words.
(The priests go out to confer and return shortly)

PRIEST OF ANI:

We, my fellow priest and I, have come back to you with our decision. We are the handmaids of the gods. You, the chiefs, make kings. You, with the kings, make the laws. We are only servants of the gods. Leave us out of state matters. Wazobia was the choice of the gods. Do not poke your finger into the eyes of the gods. Leave the priests out of this.

IYASE:

It is the people's will.

IDEHEN:

You are the servants of the people.

PRIEST OF ANI:

We are the servants of the gods. The will of the gods.

CHORUS OF MEN:

The will of the people! You serve the people!

PRIESTS:

We serve the gods!

CHORUS OF MEN:

You serve the people! The will of the people!

PRIESTS:

We serve the gods!

(The people have risen in arms. In the fray, IYASE *and* IDEHEN *force the calabash and steaming pot of herbs into the priests' hands. Battle calls are heard. War sounds. Drums increase in tempo, throbbing the sound of battle. The men rush to the palace square, chanting. "Out Wazobia, depose Wazobia, oust Wazobia." The unusual noise sets* WAZOBIA *up. She stands to see things for herself, when suddenly the men ram into her, with the priests thrusting their burden to her.* WAZOBIA *looks from side to side. She is surrounded on all sides; she feels utterly alone)*

IYASE:

Receive Wazobia, the people's present to you.

CHORUS OF MEN:

Wazobia,

The will of the people,

The people, Wazobia!

*(*WAZOBIA, *confused and frightened, looks for any*

friendly face, but she is alone. Suddenly the cock crows.
Women from behind the throne sound their war cries.
Led by the OMU, *they advance, naked and in unison,*
form an arc behind WAZOBIA. *The men are so shocked*
that they retreat, stagger, and freeze in their stupefac-
tion. Total silence. From behind, someone pushes WA
and ANEHE *forward to the front of* IYASE *and* IDEHEN *and*
the men carrying the pot of herbs and the calabash. OMU
looks with fiery eyes at them)

OMU: *(to* WA *and* ANEHE*)*
Eat from your potion! Women, that is your charge! *(The*
women advanced forward, still in their moon-shaped
formation, to lynch the treacherous women and the
men, when WAZOBIA, *standing in all her majesty, halts*
them. The men, hypnotized and disorganized, continue
their retreat)

WAZOBIA:
Women, peace! Peace! Spill no blood. Ours is to plant
seed yams. Not blood to feed worms.
Sing, women! Stand firm on the soil! Sing! Sing!
Sing, women! Plant on firm soil. Sing, women! *(The*
women take up the chorus)

OMU:
Long reign Wazobia!
(The women continue the chants, dancing and advanc-
ing until they close up and form a near-circle around
WAZOBIA. *The women join hands in their dance and*
chant, swinging their hips. Drum music increases. They
swing their hips, until music reaches fever pitch and
with WAZOBIA *in their center. They mount her shoulder-*
high and scream)
"Long reign Wa-zo-bia" *(Light lingers until final black-*
out)

BOOKS IN THE AFRICAN AMERICAN LIFE SERIES

Coleman Young and Detroit Politics: From Social Activist to Power Broker, by Wilbur Rich, 1988

Great Black Russian: A Novel on the Life and Times of Alexander Pushkin, by John Oliver Killens, 1989

Indignant Heart: A Black Worker's Journal, by Charles Denby, 1989 (reprint)

The Spook Who Sat by the Door, by Sam Greenlee, 1989 (reprint)

Roots of African American Drama: An Anthology of Early Plays, 1858–1938, edited by Leo Hamalian and James V. Hatch, 1990

Walls: Essays, 1985–1990, by Kenneth McClane, 1991

Voices of the Self: A Study of Language Competence, by Keith Gilyard, 1991

Say Amen, Brother! Old-Time Negro Preaching: A Study in American Frustration, by William H. Pipes, 1991 (reprint)

The Politics of Black Empowerment: The Tranformation of Black Activism in Urban America, by James Jennings, 1991

Pan Africanism in the African Diaspora: The African-American Linkage, by Ronald Walters, 1992

Three Plays: The Broken Calabash, Parables for a Season, and The Reign of Wazobia, by Tess Akaeke Onwueme, 1993